On Prayer

Marcel Mauss

ON PRAYER

Translated by

Susan Leslie

Edited and with an Introduction

by W.S.F. Pickering

and

Concluding Remarks

by Howard Morphy

Durkheim Press/Berghahn Books
New York • Oxford

First published in 2003 by

Berghahn Books
www.berghahnbooks.com

Reprinted in 2008

Library of Congress Cataloging-in-Publication Data

Mauss, Marcel, 1872–1950.
[La Prière. English]
On prayer : text and commentary / Marcel Mauss.
p. cm.
Includes bibliographical references.
ISBN 1-57181-633-X (alk. paper)
1. Prayer. 2. Religion and sociology. I. Title.

BL560.M3813 2003
306.6'9143--dc21

2003051812

British Library Cataloguing in Publication Data
A catalogue record for this book is available from the British Library.

Printed in the United States on acid-free paper
ISBN 978-1-57181-633-7

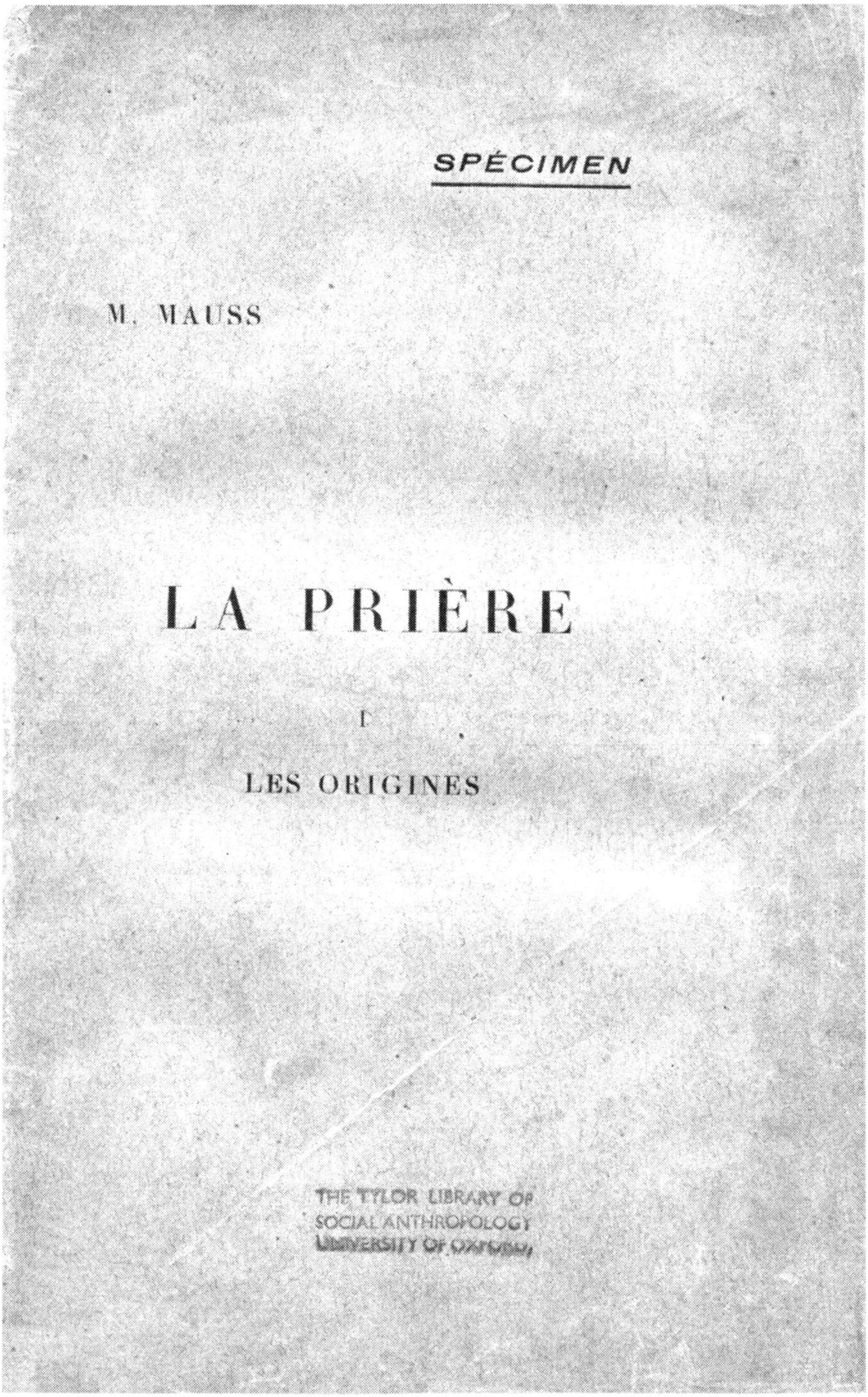

SPÉCIMEN

M. MAUSS

LA PRIÈRE

I

LES ORIGINES

A reproduction of the cover of *La Prière* printed in 1909 and privately circulated. The original is located in the Institute of Social and Cultural Anthropology, Oxford University.

Contents

Acknowledgements

The British Centre for Durkheimian Studies and the Durkheim Press, which are both located in Oxford, are grateful to M. Pierre Mauss of Montpellier for permission to translate Marcel Mauss's *La Prière*.

The Centre also wishes to thank David Roth for the financial contribution he made towards the cost of translation.

The production of this book has been essentially the co-operative venture of people who have worked on the project started several years ago. Nevertheless the Editor, who called on their services, wishes to thank them by name.

Sincere gratitude is extended to Susan Leslie for undertaking the arduous task of translation, and to Nick Allen who has assisted in dealing with technical points raised by translating such a complicated text. His advice and many comments made at nearly every stage of the development of the book have been much appreciated.

Howard Morphy, a specialist in Australian ethnography, has kindly written some observations on Mauss's work on prayer and his use and interpretation of primary sources available in his day.

A considerable contribution has been made by Robert Parkin who has closely examined the large number of sometimes complicated footnotes that Mauss spread liberally over his text.

The Editor also extends warm thanks to Dominique Lussier, Julia Goddard and his wife, Carol, who in various ways have helped in the production of the manuscript.

W.S.F.P.

Presentation, Notes and Referencing

The use of italicized words, especially those of proper names, seems to follow no rule in Mauss's text. For translation purposes, it was decided to keep the original italicization.

At the bottom of several pages of the text by Mauss, there are footnotes contributed by N.J. Allen. To differentiate them from Mauss's numbered notes, they are designated by * and †. Mauss's own notes are given at the end of his text.

In the Introduction and concluding contribution by Howard Morphy, a reference such as (p.73) denotes the page-number of the English translation of *La Prière* presented here.

Introduction to an Unfinished Work

W.S.F. Pickering

It is a remarkable fact that prayer as a subject on its own has scarcely been studied by anthropologists, let alone by sociologists. Mauss's work on the subject makes him one of the few scholars with anthropological interests who have tackled it.[1] In this, as in other ways, he stands out as a pioneer.

Marcel Mauss, born in 1872, was the nephew of Emile Durkheim (1858–1917). As the founder in France of sociology as a university discipline in the late nineteenth century, Durkheim's later influence spread far and wide. Both men were born in Epinal in Lorraine and both were agnostic, with a deep-rooted Jewish family background. Further, they shared a common and sensitive interest in religion (Pickering 1984; 1998). This is apparent not least in this little-known but important study Mauss made of prayer, which is translated here into English for the first time.

Mauss's work on prayer was to have constituted a doctoral thesis. However, the completing of theses was something of a *bête noire* to him. While he was at Bordeaux University, finishing his *agrégation* in philosophy under the patriarchal eye of his uncle, he had decided that when he went to Paris to study for a doctorate, his minor thesis – his Latin thesis – would be on Spinoza, the philosopher of Jewish origin, and his relation to Leo the Hebrew (Mauss 1979).[2] In fact when he came to Paris in 1895 with this in mind, he abandoned it two years later, having met a M. Couchoud who seems to have undermined his resolve (ibid.). For some time before, Mauss had decided to study philology, including Semitic languages and religion, in the Ecole Pratique des Hautes Etudes, Vth section, which had as its aim the scientific study of religion – *les sciences religieuses*. Optimistically he thought that here he could write his major thesis, which was at first called 'Sur les Origines de la prière', in the matter of a few years. That also was never finished. Such blemishes on his academic career were taken with him to the grave. But here he was not alone. At least one other devotee of Durkheim did no better, brilliant scholar though he was. This was Henri Hubert who died in 1927. It may also be recalled that Robert Hertz never completed his doctorate. Killed in World War I at the age of 33, he had had difficulty in deciding on a topic (Parkin 1996:3–4). Both these men were colleagues and close friends of Mauss.

Wrestling with the thesis

What were the events surrounding Mauss's failure to complete his thesis? In 1897, two years after he had been in Paris, Durkheim suggested that Emile Boutroux (1845–1921), a philosopher and friend, should be asked to help Mauss with a 'projet ferme' (Durkheim 1998a:53). Nothing, however, seems to have come of this and things were obviously not going well for the thesis. Mauss, however, thought that a visit to such countries as Holland and England would be helpful, for he would be able to meet scholars interested in *la science des religions* (Durkheim 1998a:62). His first visit to England came in 1898 but his uncle urged him to cut it short, implying that he might be wasting his time.

For some time Mauss had immersed himself in reading ethnographic studies of the Australian Aboriginals. The research led to work which was subsequently incorporated into Durkheim's great book, *The Elementary Forms of Religious Life* (1912a). But it was also material that was necessary for his own thesis. Mauss gave two courses of lectures on prayer at the Ecole Pratique des Hautes Etudes in 1901 and 1902, in which he doubtless used material destined for the thesis. In all this he was encouraged by his colleagues (Fournier 1994:333). Apart from a short visit to North Africa, taken late in life, Mauss was an arm-chair anthropologist, and all the major ethnographic material he used in the thesis came from the writings of fieldworkers such as B. Spencer, F. J. Gillen and others (see Morphy 1998).

So it was that in 1909, some 12 years at least after Mauss had started the thesis, and when he was 37 years of age, he decided to publish its opening sections (*Livres*). The first was a general introduction and the second, 'Nature des rites oraux élémentaires' was based on Australian ethnographic material (1909).[3] According to the copies that have been handed down to us, it was 176 pages long and was privately printed by Alcan, who also published nearly all the books of the Durkheimians. In fact only a few copies, six it is said, appeared. Along with studies on other aspects of the life of the Australian Aboriginals, these pages were the sole result of many years' work which brought him at first great hope and then much suffering (Fournier 1994:331). Mauss had submitted to Durkheim the draft of the first two parts of the thesis but Durkheim was very unhappy about what he read. Espinas, who had preceded

Durkheim in Bordeaux and was now in Paris, liked the method Mauss adopted. However, Durkheim wanted Sylvain Lévi, his supervisor, to decide the outcome. That sealed its fate, and there were no more copies. The few copies available were not widely circulated. The cover was marked 'Specimen'. (see Frontispiece here) What he published in this abortive work represented, he said, only about a fourth of the planned thesis (Mauss 1979/t.1983:148). He intended to write about oral rites amongst the Aborginals of Australia, Melanesia and Polynesia, as well as about similar rites in Vedic India, among Semites and early Christians (ibid.). Such a task seemed doomed by its very ambition.

What appears to have caused Mauss serious hesitation in pursuing the thesis was the new ethnographic material concerning the Australian Aboriginals, produced by Carl Strehlow, which came to Mauss's attention just at the time that he published the opening part of his thesis. It had much bearing on his argument over the question of whether prayer was or was not found among the Arunta. Mauss raised this issue in the second part of what was published. In 1912 he was still trying to unravel problems relating to Strehlow's work (see *L'Année sociologique*, XII:445–8; Fournier 1994:340). Incidentally Durkheim referred very frequently and approvingly to the work of Strehlow in *Les Formes élémentaires* (1912a). Mauss continued giving lectures on the Aboriginals and their oral rites well into the 1920s. But no matter what all the circumstances surrounding the thesis were, it was meant to be 'his great work' (Fournier 1994:331). As such it never appeared.

Whatever Mauss may have written in addition to what has been handed down to us, for example about prayer in Hinduism and among Semitic peoples, has never come to light, nor has the correspondence he had with Strehlow. Yet it is believed that much existed at one time, perhaps in note form as lectures given to students. It should not be imagined, however, that Mauss's interests in prayer were confined solely to the thesis. Karady in the *Œuvres* presents 13 items, which he categorizes as 'Notes'. These include references to prayer in reviews by Mauss, although they also refer to other subjects such as the notion of a primitive people (*Œuvres* I:478–524). Then there are 'Textes' collected by Karady which undergird his thesis (ibid.:525–48). Here there are firm allusions to prayer and allied matters. So Mauss's introduction to his anticipated thesis has remained in the background for many decades. He never referred to it in his subsequent writings. He did not wish, it seems, that people should know about it. Cazeneuve, who gave the work considerable coverage in his small book on Mauss written in 1968, also stresses that Mauss makes scarcely any reference to it in his other writings, although it is a fact that Mauss seldom referred back to any earlier works (1968:76). It is seldom referred to by scholars, whether anthropologists, historians or theologians (ibid.:77).[4] It is also notably the case with Lévi-Strauss who promoted Mauss's work. However, one person who gave it some prominence was the anthropologist, Maurice Leenhardt, in his obituary of Mauss (Leenhardt 1950–1). Other works by Mauss of great pioneering merit later overshadowed it, for example, 'Essai sur le don'(1925), 'Les Techniques du corps' (1935) and 'La Personne' (1938). At least it has been brought more to the attention of a wider public by its inclusion in Karady's *Œuvres* of Mauss which appeared in 1968. But despite that, no scholar appears to have dealt with it in any depth. Although Marcel Fournier has recently described in detail the background against which it was written, he gives less place to its contents (Fournier 1993:331–41).

It is rather astonishing, then, that the findings of a German ethnographer should have brought Mauss's work to a complete stop, and at a point where, according to his own plans, he was just opening up the thesis. What was printed comes to a very abrupt end. That in itself seems strange. Leenhardt readily accepts that the reason for the thesis having never been finished was because of Strehlow's new findings (Leenhardt 1950–1). But one wonders. It seems extraordinary that more could not have been published, not least because Mauss had so much knowledge on the subject, quite apart from the Australian controversy. Did everything really depend on this particular ethnographic report? The reason for the final decision to guillotine the publication, which rested with Lévi, remains a mystery. Mauss alone knew the answer. He died in 1950. In the last chapter of this book Morphy offers a plausible answer. He argues that as Mauss progressed, he became overwhelmed with new and extensive ethnographic material which conflicted with what he had already written. He further hints that Mauss may also have found that prayer as a general concept was difficult to handle.

Other factors, however, might well have been at work.

Personal factors: the influence and demands of Durkheim

A case might be presented where Mauss's failure to finish his thesis was due not so much to intellectual inabilites as to his personality and to matters arising from his relationship with his uncle. The abruptness points to some psychological factor, though precisely what it was is very difficult to determine. All one can do is to point to certain facets of his character and personal relations.

Through the recent publication of a book of letters from Durkheim to Mauss, we know more about the background of the saga of non-completion than heretofore (see Durkheim 1998a). It is patently obvious that Mauss did not possess that fixity of purpose and resolve that was found in his serious-minded, professionally oriented uncle. Many were the occasions, we now read, when the uncle chided the nephew for a lack of determination and his poor self-discipline, which prevented him from making progress in writing his major thesis (see, for example, Durkheim 1998a:31 and 129). In 1898 he wrote:

'Mais il y a une chose à laquelle tu es strictement tenu, c'est à faire ta thèse. Tu te le dois par dignité, tu nous le dois' (ibid.:124). And again later in 1907: 'Ne crains-tu pas le ridicule de l'homme qui prépare éternellement un livre qui n'aboutit pas – ridicule encore accru par la sévèrité outrée que tu témoignes pour les travaux d'autrui' (ibid.:387). Earlier, Durkheim had tried to encourage him by suggesting that he, Durkheim, could help him with the thesis. It would be of mutual aid because any ethnographic material Mauss might have unearthed would have been of assistance to Durkheim (ibid.:124). He warned his nephew that if his lack of productivity could not be overcome, he was destined to be a 'mediocre' professor at a lycée all his life (ibid.). Durkheim wrote in another letter in 1898: 'Tes ambitions sont éteintes. ... Sois un jeune homme, et non un retraité avant l'âge' (ibid.:119). 'Ta thèse Dieu sait quand' (ibid:134). (Appropiate words for a thesis on prayer!).

Durkheim was of the opinion that the 'Essai sur la nature et la fonction du sacrifice' which Mauss wrote in conjunction with Henri Hubert took Mauss away from his prime target, the completion of the thesis, important though the publication was (ibid.:149). The essay appeared in 1898 and has many parallels with *La Prière*.

It would seem that while undertaking research, Mauss was in fact asked to be a teacher in a lycée, and Durkheim, along with Mauss's widowed mother, wrote that he should not accept such an appointment (ibid.:128). Not unexpectedly, his mother was always urging him to finish the thesis and offered to help him financially (see Fournier 1993:334). In 1930, relatively late in life, he became professor at the Collège de France. It seems remarkable from what we know of his academic achievements in terms of teaching and producing learned and creative articles that there was a time when he might have spent the rest of his life as a teacher in a remote lycée. In the call for Mauss to work harder and to be better disciplined, Durkheim himself was not blameless. He made enormous demands on his nephew. For example, he asked him to write innumerable reviews for the *Année sociologique*, the very important journal Durkheim founded in 1896 and subsequently directed. He expected him to perform other tasks such as reading ethnographic material and preparing tables of statistics on suicide, which were of benefit to Durkheim himself. Also, when Durkheim was in Bordeaux and Mauss in Paris, he was goaded by his uncle into corresponding with him more regularly. The fact remains that all Durkheim's efforts to persuade his nephew to be a serious-minded professional like himself failed.

Academic interest in the subject of prayer

Although Mauss, as we have noted, was unique among anthropologists and sociologists who studied prayer as a subject in itself – and the Durkheimians did not distinguish the two disciplines in those days – it must not be thought that prayer was a subject seldom considered by academics at that time. Since the object of this introduction is not so much to expound the contents of the text as to set it within the academic and personal context in which it was written, it seems apposite to refer to other academics who wrote on the subject of prayer at about this time.

Around the turn of the century there was indeed a rich seam of studies by theologians, philosophers of religion and church historians who were attempting to apply objective, 'scientific' approaches to religious phenomena in which prayer was seen as a significant component. They used the approaches of critical history, original languages, psychology, and comparative studies. Many of those writing at the *fin de siècle* were Germans, such as E. von der Goltz, H. Engert, P. Drews, and O. Dibelius. Mauss read them all and praised Goltz in particular for he was one of the few who attempted a scientific history of Christian prayer, coupled with a sociological approach. He lacked, however, a theory of the origins of prayer and was too theological (Mauss 1903:212; 215–6). Mauss was opposed to much of the work of theologians and philosophers, and in his own day he attacked the writings of the Dutch scholar Cornelius Tiele and the Frenchman, Auguste Sabatier. To these scholars we now turn very briefly since today their work is probably forgotten.

Tiele and Sabatier

Cornelius Tiele was born in 1830 and died in 1902. He was a Dutch Remonstrant pastor and a theologian who became a professor at Leiden. He was a specialist in the languages and history of the Near East and an authority on comparative religion. His work was not only influential in Holland but also in the Ecole Pratique des Hautes Etudes. He gave the Gifford Lectures in Edinburgh in 1896 and 1898 under the title *Elements of the Science of Religion* (1897–9) (see the review by Mauss 1899a and 1900). A key component of religion is worship, and in worship prayer is 'the most important element' (1897–9,II:133). In the end the essence of religion could not be determined by the findings of science. What is superhuman, he argued, falls outside the range of what is perceptible and therefore could not be proved or disproved by science or philosophy (ibid. I:4–5). Mauss was critical of Tiele: he was too philosophical and not scientific enough, and his evolutionary idea of the way the notion of God developed was too simple (Mauss 1900:547).

Auguste Sabatier (1839–1901) was a French Protestant pastor and theologian who became a professor in Strasbourg, which he left on account of the German annexation of Alsace after the 1870 war. Eventually, in 1877, he helped to create the Protestant Faculty of Theology in Paris, of which he was subsequently the dean. Keen on reforming the church, he strongly supported the ideas of Schleiermacher and Ritschl and was influential in the Ecole Pratique des Hautes Etudes. In many ways he paved the way for the growth of

Modernism amongst Protestants in France, as well as among Catholics. His best known book was *Esquisse d'une philosophie de la religion d'après la psychologie et l'histoire*, published in 1897 (see the review by Mauss of 1898). For him religion was based on a sense of mystery which he held to be universal. This was coupled with the notion that the individual was faced with the problem of his destiny. Religion was thus the conscious relation between the soul in distress and the mysterious power outside the individual. This relation was realized through prayer. 'C'est la prière qui distingue le phénomène religieux de tous ce qui lui ressemblent ou l'avoisinent, tels que le sentiment moral ou le sentiment esthétique'. Hence prayer becomes the criterion for deciding what is religious. Not surprisingly Sabatier attacked the notion of 'natural' religion because, according to him, it deprived people of prayer.

The one thing that Mauss, Tiele and Sabatier had in common was an alleged commitment to *les sciences religieuses*. Under this rubric it was possible to study religion in the Sorbonne, for in the University it was located in the Ecole Pratique des Hautes Etudes, Fifth Section (see Strenski 1997). *Les sciences religieuses* constituted an approach to the study of religious life and religious institutions which was intended to be free from theological dogmatism or confessional interpretation. 'Facts' about religions were the chief priority – the study of ancient languages and texts, coupled with historical and textual criticism. The next stage was to try to explain the facts. And so psychology, anthropology and sociology entered the field.

It was said, however, that some scholars moved beyond facts and transgressed the canons of science. Their personal beliefs entered the academic forum. Thus, starting with *les sciences religieuses*, they tended to project their own beliefs about, for example, Christianity and the nature of religion. Their standpoint was essentially Western, even when studying Eastern religions. It can be seen, for example, in Tiele: 'Yet one thing is certain, religion dwells in the inmost depths of our souls ... Our religion is ourselves, in so far as we raise ourselves above the finite and transient' (1897–9 II:24). On the whole these scholars were evolutionist, some seeing Christianity as the most developed form of religion. Modernism or religious liberalism became convenient words to label the endeavours of such scholars who often rejected or radically modified traditional dogma. Apart from liberal Protestant and Jewish scholars, some of whom have been mentioned, the most prominent of the Catholics were Le Roy, Laberthonnière, Blondel and Loisy. Duschene, the historian, was somewhat on the fringe. The hope of many of these scholars was that by accepting the use of scientific methods, religion and indeed Christianity would be more acceptable to those intellectuals who had rejected traditional Christian doctrine and practice.

One solution to the problem of holding on to a religious faith, while at the same time accepting the findings of *les sciences religieuses*, was to make the core of religion rest on experience. For Sabatier this was seen as the subjective realization of the mystery between the 'I' and a universal cause (1897 I:viii). But much Modernism if taken to its logical conclusion tends to reduce religion to ethics and nothing more. However some scholars such as Sabatier parried this position, holding that religious experience transcends ethics. Nevertheless in practice, Modernists in the spirit of Kant, placed great emphasis on the moral.

What were the reactions of the Durkheimians to Modernism? Strenski quite rightly accuses Durkheim and his followers of wanting to have it both ways. Assuredly they held that the facts were of prime importance, but the theories of the Durkheimians have often been seen to be reductionist to a social domain, where the social and not the individual is the methodological starting-point (Strenski 1998). Of course the Durkheimians were at home in an academic centre which studied religion without dogmatic censure and where *les sciences religieuses* were the foundation of their studies. One might have thought they would have favoured Modernism. In general, however, this was not the case as Mauss states in his work on prayer and as we have mentioned. Modernists were seen to be compromisers who accepted 'science' only half-heartedly. With one or two exceptions all of the Durkheimians were agnostic, if not atheist. Their rationalist humanism prevented any compromise with religious 'truths', especially in cases where these were intertwined with apologetics. As we have hinted, the alleged objectivity of Modernist scholars was undermined by their ultimate goal of being 'on the side of religion'. It remains true that many of their attempts to universalise religious phenomena – for example, to say that certain tribes had beliefs which were close to the Christian concept of God – do in fact show a firm pro-Christian bias. This was frequently bound up with a particular evolutionary approach which asserted that, starting with primitive societies, one could see something of a divine plan which made Christianity a kind of omega point, where earlier religions prepared the ground for the final 'revelation' (*Œuvres* I:533).[5] *Mutatis mutandis* this view was supported by some scholars in the decades that followed the First World War and extended into the 1950s, for example, E.O. James (1888–1972), the doyen of comparative religion in Britain in this period. He saw that his task was to reconcile the growth of 'scientific' knowledge of religion with the notion of divine revelation.

However, while the Durkheimians were critical of Modernism, they kept a low profile. The reason was political. Liberal Protestants, as has been noted, dominated the Ecole Pratique in its early days. Durkheimians wanted a secure and influential place in the Ecole. Consequently they decided that it was unwise, until they had firmly established themselves there, to go on the attack, particularly against Auguste Sabatier and Albert Réville (Strenski 2000).

Friedrich Heiler

The brief allusion to an interest in prayer by scholars in Mauss's day prompts one to recall that the trend would extend beyond World War I. In 1918 Heiler's

Das Gebet appeared and became something of a classic. Friedrich Heiler was born in 1892. Brought up a Roman Catholic, he became a High Church Lutheran and held a number of academic posts in theology in Germany.

The book displayed some ideas similar to those of Mauss. It seems, however, certain that Heiler would not have read Mauss's work. Nevertheless they both made their starting-point the phenomenon of prayer as a universal component of religion. The initial approach, historical and anthropological, was structured around a developmental and evolutionary framework. They both began by examining the most primitive forms and saw the culmination of prayer in the mysticism of the individual.

The two authors held that prayer was not only universal or almost universal, but that it could be said to be the essence of religion – its central point. Heiler quoted approvingly from many writers to support his contention ([1918] 1932:xiii). Not surprisingly the two scholars differed radically in terms of emphasis and analysis. For Heiler the individual is always prior to the social. 'Prayer is ... a living communion of the religious man with God, conceived as personal and present in experience, a communion which reflects the forms of the social realms of humanity' (ibid.:358). Heiler's traditional Christian background encouraged him to see that prayer is at the core of that tradition. Prayer is the communion of an individual with his god, and contains an emotional strand. Thus he could write: 'Genuine prayer is the free, spontaneous expression of one's own experience, or at least the fruit of what one has experienced and gained in struggle' (ibid.:xxii). It is only towards the end of the book that Heiler considers prayer in public worship. Ritual for Heiler is all too easily associated with the primitive and hence with magic.

As Mauss turns to anthropology for an analysis of prayer, so Heiler, like other scholars mentioned above, turns to psychology. The subtitle of the book is *A Study in the History and Psychology of Religion*. Psychology was more acceptable to theologians and Christian intellectuals since its starting-point was the individual or the soul. By contrast the impersonality and coldness attributed to the social, and therefore to sociology and anthropology, introduced a note of the mechanical and smelled of determinism. This is seen as being contrary to the Christian doctrine of man. In searching for motives for prayer, Heiler adopted the common position of his day by asserting that the first prayers came through fear, need, calamity, and the search for food. Such simple explanations or original causes were strongly rejected by Durkheim and Mauss. 'Absolute' origins are impossible to discover.

The most developed form of prayer, mysticism, Heiler sees as 'the flight of the alone to the Alone'. Its deep psychological roots are for him obvious. As a Lutheran, however, he is ambivalent towards mysticism, since it does not need any mediation between man and God and the work of Jesus Christ thus becomes superfluous.

The Psychology of Prayer: Segond's thesis

Since the issue of a psychological approach to prayer has been raised, it is worthwhile pursuing it a little further.

It is interesting to note that two years after Mauss let the introduction to his incomplete thesis be known to his friends, Joseph Segond was examined for a doctoral thesis on the subject by a jury, one member of which was Emile Durkheim. What happened at the *soutenance* is of interest, not least because of Durkheim's many interventions (Durkheim 1911e) and Mauss's later review of the published thesis.

Durkheim vigorously attacked Segond's thesis from positions most apparent in Mauss's work. His criticism was along two lines. First, the method adopted by the examinee was subjective and relied on the personal experiences of individuals. He held that collective mental states were nothing but 'the echo in diverse individual *consciences* of social influences' (in Lukes 1973:658). Second, Segond gave only limited attention to primitive forms, not least because in early societies, for example Australian tribes, some observers doubted the existence of prayer.

Segond's focus was on mysticism, which he held to be the highest form of prayer, and Durkheim noted that such a form had limitations for objective study. Mystics relied entirely on feeling, on an awareness of the transcendence of the self in communicating directly with a Beyond. In the end, prayer becomes a silence and the subjective element of prayer the most profound of all its elements. Echoing Mauss's position, Durkheim also criticised Segond for his failure to treat prayer in terms of ritual. As is obvious, Segond's thesis was very much in line with Protestant modernism. Perhaps he himself was a Protestant.[6]

And what of Mauss's review of Segond's thesis? (The review has been translated here.) Not surprisingly it is far from complimentary for it reflects Durkheim's comments just stated, and shows Mauss's distance from liberal Protestantism (Mauss 1913). Although, says Mauss, Segond took account of Durkheimian methodology, he made no real contribution to it and indeed did not understand it. He failed to see what effect prayer had on the one who prays (surely there is a concession here to a psychological approach on the part of Mauss?). Like his uncle, Mauss attacked Segond's emphasis on mysticism and his positing the existence of a being superior to the individual soul.

Disagreement with received anthropological thought: prayer and incantation

Although Mauss was no doubt influenced by, and at the same time criticized liberal Protestant theologians and historians on the subject of prayer, he also challenged anthropologists and historians of religion of his day who, while not treating it as a subject in its own right, showed some limited interest in it. Nevertheless he disagreed with them on several counts.

The origin of prayer, in the eyes of Müller, Marett and Rivers, was to be found at a late stage in the evolution of religion. It had emerged from the earlier stage of magic where individuals did not pray but incanted, that is, uttered spells and charms within the context of magic. Incantation was differentiated from prayer, as magic was from religion.

Prayer implies something non-mechanical, personal – a human plea, for example – which might or might not be granted by the supernatural being to whom the prayer was being addressed. It assumed that the deity had personal characteristics, by which the outcome could be decided. But it also might be a freely expressed word of praise or thanksgiving addressed to a god. By contrast magic contains an element of causality – a kind of primitive scientific action whereby, if the right words are spoken and correct actions carried out, the result is inevitable. Such prayers can be designated incantations and are associated with charms and spells. Efficacity depends on using the right formula or the correct ritual action.

Mauss (and Durkheim) challenged some of the assumptions in these dichotomies. The matter could only be settled, as Durkheim implied in *Les Formes élémentaires* (1912a), by examining the most primitive tribes known to mankind, which they both thought were the Australian Aboriginals. Crawley and Schmidt, who had not worked in the field, thought that the Australians indeed used incantation but not prayer. And those who did undertake fieldwork, such as Howitt, Spencer and Gillen, agreed. However, Mrs Parker, also an early ethnographer, believed that what they uttered were real prayers, that is, they were addressed to a spiritual being. To this issue of prayer versus incantation – invocation versus evocation – Mauss devoted Book II of his introduction in analysing the ethnographic writings of others who worked in the field. He disagreed with both schools of interpretation and tried to show that the Aboriginals referred to spiritual beings and would therefore both pray and use magic spells, the two actions existing side by side. (see the last chapter here by Morphy).

Main issues outlined

It is beyond the scope of this introduction to analyse the main arguments of Mauss's thesis as it has come down to us. There will doubtless be those who find his general introduction to prayer insightful, stimulating and a firm rebuttal of the notion that prayer is essentially a personal or individual phenomenon. Others, however, will view his work as being outmoded and of little value in anthropological fieldwork. The point is that *La Prière* speaks to people of several disciplines and interests.

Notes

1. An exception in recent years has been the work of Stephen Headley 1994, 1996, and Parkin and Headley 2000. Ses also articles in *L'Homme*, 34, 1994. Of course, earlier scholars, such Frazer and later Marett considered the subject but within limits.
2. See also in a revised English translation of Mauss 1979 in James and Allen 1998:35.
3. *La Prière* may be found in Karady's *Marcel Mauss: Œuvres*, I:357–477. (See Mauss 1968–9). Karady omits the last page.
4. One exception is to be seen in Allen 1985.
5. This position has overtones in the concept of the Omega Point in the work of Teilhard de Chardin.
6. Joseph Segond may have been related to Louis Segond, a biblical exegete, who was born in 1810 and died in 1885. In 1880 he produced a highly acclaimed translation of the Bible in French, which was published in Oxford as well as in France. Incidentally Joseph Segond (1872–1954) became Professor of Philosophy in Aix-Marseille and wrote a number of books on a range of philosophical and psychological subjects. His main concern, however, was to expound and develop the thought of Bergson.

References

Allen, N.J. [1985] 2000 'The Category of the Person: a reading of Mauss's last essay', in N. J. Allen, *Categories and Classifications. Maussian Reflection on the Social*, New York, Oxford: Berghahn Books.

Besnard, P. (ed.) 1983 *The Sociological Domain. The Durkheimians and the founding of French sociology*, Cambridge: Cambridge University Press.

Cazeneuve, J. 1968 *Sociologie de Marcel Mauss*, Paris: Presses Universitaires de France.

Durkheim, E. 1911e Examination of thesis. J. Segond, *La Prière. Etude psychologique religieuse, Revue de métaphysique et de morale*, XIX, supplément janvier, pp.32–3. t.1968e in Lukes 1973:657–61.

Durkheim, E. 1912a *Les Formes élémentaires de la vie religieuse*, Paris: Alcan.

Durkheim, E. 1998a *Lettres à Marcel Mauss*, Presentées par P. Besnard et M. Fournier, Paris: Presses Universitaires de France.

Fournier, M. 1994 *Marcel Mauss*, Paris: Fayard.

Headley, S. 1994 'Pour une anthropologie de la prière', *L'Homme*, 34:7–14.

Headley, S. 1996 *Vers une anthropologie de la prière; études ethnolinguistiques javanaises*, 3 vols, Aix-en-Provence: Publications de l'Université de Provence.

Heiler, F. [1918] 1932 *Prayer. A Study in the History and Psychology of Religion*, New York: Oxford University Press. (It is an abbreviation and English translation by S. McComb and J. Park of the original, *Das Gebet. Eine religionsgeschichtlicte und religionspsychologische Unteruchung.*

James, W. and Allen, N.J. (eds) 1998 *Marcel Mauss: A Centenary Tribute*, New York and Oxford: Berghahn Books.

Karady, V. 1968 Note de l'Editeur, *La Prière*, Mauss 1968–9, I:356.

Leenhardt, M. 1950–1 'Marcel Mauss (1872–1950)', in *Annuaire*, Paris: Ecole Pratique des Hautes Etudes, Section des Sciences Religieuses.

Lukes, S. 1973 *Emile Durkheim. His Life and Work: A Historical and Intellectual Study*, London: Allen Lane.

Mauss, M. 1898 Review. A Sabatier, *Esquisse d'une philosophie de la religion d'après la psychologie et l'histoire*, Paris, 1897, *L'Année sociologique*, I:171–77. Reproduced in *Œuvres*, I:531–6.
Mauss, M. 1899a Review. P. Tiele, *Inleiding tot de Godsdienst Wetenschap (Gifford Lezingen)*, Part I, English translation, *Elements of the Science of Religion*, *L'Année sociologique* II:187–93. Reproduced in *Œuvres* I:539–345.
Mauss, M. 1899b Review. F. Coblenz, *Über das betende Ich der Psalmen*, *L'Année sociologique*, II:266. Reproduced in *Œuvres*, I:484–5.
Mauss, M. 1900 Review. J.C.P. Tiele, *Elements of the Science of Religion*, Part II, *L'Année sociologique*. III:195–8. Reproduced in *Œuvres*, I:539–45.
Mauss, M. 1903 Review. E. von der Goltz, *Das Gebet in der ältesten Christenheit*, Leipzig, 1901, *L'Année sociologique*, VI:211–7. Reproduced in *Œuvres*, I:478–83.
Mauss, M. 1904 Review. O. Dibelius *Das Vaterunser, Umrisse zu einer Geschichte des Gebets in der alten und mittleren Kirche*, 1903, *L'Année sociologique* VII:304–8, Reproduced in *Œuvres* I:485–9.
Mauss, M. 1909 *La Prière*, Paris. Reproduced in *Œuvres* I:357–477. [Last page missing]
Mauss, M. 1913 Review. J. Segond, *La Prière. Essai de psychologie religieuse*, *L'Année sociologique*, XII:239–40.
Mauss, M. 1925 'Essai sur le don, forme et raison de l'échange dans les sociétés archaiques', *L'Année sociologique*, n.s. 1:30–186.
Mauss, M. 1935 'Les Techniques du corps', *Journal de psychologie normal et pathologique*, 32:271–93.
Mauss, M. 1968–9 *Marcel Mauss: Œuvres*, 3 vols, présentation de Victor Karady, Paris: Les Editions de Minuet.
Mauss 1979 'L'Œuvre de Mauss par lui-même', *Revue française de sociologie*, XX, 1:209–20. Translated into English in Besnard 1983 and revised in James and Allen 1998.
Morphy, H. 1998 'Spencer and Gillen in Durkheim: the theoretical construction of ethnography', in N.J. Allen, W.S.F. Pickering and W. Watts Miller (eds) *On Durkheim's Elementary Forms of Religious Life*, London: Routledge.
Œuvres, see Mauss 1968–9.
Parkin, D and Headley, (eds) 2000 *Islamic Prayer across the Indian Ocean: inside and outside the Mosque*, Richmond, UK: Curzon.
Parkin, R. 1996 *The Dark Side of Humanity. The Work of Robert Hertz and its Legacy*, Australia: Harwood Academic.
Pickering, W.S.F. 1984 *Durkheim's Sociology of Religion: Themes and Theories*, London: Routledge and Kegan Paul.
Sabatier, A. 1897 *Esquisse d'une philosophie de la religion d'après la psychologie et l'histoire*, Paris: Fischbacher.
Strenski, I. 1997 *Durkheim and the Jews of France*, Chicago and London: University of Chicago Press.
Strenski, I. 1998 'The Ironies of *fin-de-siècle* rebellions against historicism and empiricism in the Ecole Pratique des Hautes Etudes, Fifth Section', in A. Molendijk and P. Pels (eds) *Religion in the Making*, Leiden: Brill.
Strenski, I. 2000 'Durkheimians and Protestants in the Ecole Pratique, Fifth Section, the dark side', *Durkheimian Studies/Etudes Durkheimiennes*, n.s., 6:105–14.
Tiele, C.P. 1897–9 *Elements of the Science of Religion*, 2 vols, Edinburgh and London: Blackwood.

Marcel Mauss

ON PRAYER

First published in French in 1909 as *La Prière*, Paris: pp. 1–196. Reproduced in V. Karady (ed.), 1968, *Marcel Mauss. Oeuvres*, Paris: Editions de Minuet, vol.1, pp. 357–477 (last page missing).

BOOK I

Chapter 1

General Introduction

Of all religious phenomena, there are few which, even when considered merely from the outside, give such an immediate impression of life, richness and complexity as does the phenomenon of prayer. Prayer has a marvellous history. Coming from the depths, it has gradually raised itself to the heights of religious life. Infinitely supple, it has taken the most varied forms, by turns adoring and coercive, humble and threatening, dry and full of imagery, immutable and variable, mechanical and mental. It has filled the most varied roles: here it is a brusque demand, there an order, elsewhere a contract, an act of faith, a confession, a supplication, an act of praise, a hosanna. Sometimes the same type of prayer has passed successively through all the vicissitudes: almost empty at first, one sort suddenly becomes full of meaning, while another, almost sublime to start with, gradually deteriorates into mechanical psalmody.

One can easily see how interesting it might be to study and follow all the variations of something so complex and so constantly changing. It provides us with a particularly good opportunity of showing how the same institution can fulfil the most diverse functions, how the same reality can take on multiple forms while still being itself and without changing its nature.[1] Now this double aspect of social and religious things has too often been misunderstood. Sometimes they are regarded merely as simple concepts, of an abstract simplicity easily accessible to reason. Sometimes they are thought to be desperately complex and beyond the reach of reason. In reality everything social is both simple and complex. It is on material that is both concrete and in constant motion that the sociologist's abilities of abstraction are employed and legitimately employed. A study of prayer will usefully illustrate this principle.

Yet it is not only for exterior reasons that prayer should command our attention, but above all because of its very great intrinsic importance. From several aspects it is in fact one of the central phenomena of religious life.

In the first place, prayer is the point of convergence of a great number of religious phenomena. More than any other organized body of material, it partakes at the same time of the nature of ritual and the nature of belief. It is a rite because it is an assumed attitude – an action carried out with regard to sacred things. It addresses itself to the divinity and influences it; it consists of physical actions from which results are expected. But at the same time, every prayer is always to some extent a *Credo*. Even where constant use has emptied it of meaning, it still gives expression to a minimum of religious ideas and feelings. In prayer the faithful both act and think. And action and thought are closely combined, welling up in the same religious occasion, at one and the same time. Moreover, this convergence is quite natural. Prayer is speech. Now language is an activity that has an aim and effect; it is always, basically, an instrument of action. But it acts by expressing ideas and feelings that are externalized and given substance by words. To speak is both to act and to think: that is why prayer gives rise to belief and ritual at the same time.

This characteristic of prayer encourages one to study it. It is well known how difficult it is to explain a rite which is nothing but a rite, or a myth which is little else than a myth.[2] A rite only gains its *raison d'être* when one has discovered its meaning, that is, the ideas on which it is and has been based – the beliefs to which it corresponds. A myth is not really explained until one has said to which actions and rites it is linked, what are the practices to which it gives rise. On the one hand, the myth has scarcely any reality if it is not attached to some definite ritual practice; and, on the other hand, a rite has hardly any value if it is not the expression of certain beliefs. A religious idea which is detached from practices in which it functions, is something vague and imprecise. And a practice whose meaning is not known, or known from a reliable source is, from the scientific point of view, no more than a mechanical series of traditional movements, whose role cannot be determined except quite hypothetically. Normally, it is precisely myths and rituals in virtual isolation that are the subject of comparative studies in myth and ritual. We have scarcely begun to study these phenomena in which cognition (*représentation*) and action are intimately connected and whose analysis can be so fruitful. Prayer is precisely one of these phenomena where ritual is united in belief. It is full of meaning like a myth: it is often as rich in ideas and images as a religious narrative. It is full of power and efficacy like a ritual and it is often as powerfully creative as a ceremony based on sympathetic magic. At least initially, when it is composed, it is not done in a blind way: it is never something inert. So a prayer-ritual is a whole, comprising the mythical and ritual elements necessary to its understanding. One can even say that a single prayer contains several elements of self-justification, often clearly expressed. In other forms of ritual, the body of ideas and sentiments usually remains rather vague; in the case of prayer, on the contrary, the demands of language are such that often the prayer itself will specify the precise circumstances and motives which give rise to it. The analysis of prayer is therefore easier than that of most religious phenomena.

For this very reason the study of prayer will enable us to throw some light on the very controversial question of the relationship between myth and ritual. What gave rise to the debate was the fact that each of the two schools, the ritualist[3] and the mythologist, held as axiomatic that one of these elements preceded the other. Consequently, the whole problem was reduced to discovering which of the two was the religious principle *par excellence*. Now in fact every rite necessarily corresponds to a more or less vague idea and every belief gives rise to actions, however slight. But it is above all in prayer that the solidarity of these two sets of facts is strikingly obvious. Here, strictly speaking, the ritual side and the mythical side are but two aspects of one and the same action. They appear simultaneously and are inseparable. Of course science can abstract them in order to facilitate their study, but to abstract is not the same as to separate. Above all there can be no question of attributing any sort of primacy to one or to the other.

Secondly, prayer is a central phenomenon in the sense that it is one of the best signs indicating the stage of advancement of a religion. For throughout the whole course of evolution, the destinies of prayer and religion are seen to be closely linked. The history of almost all other rites consists in a continual regression. There are clusters of facts which have almost entirely disappeared, such as the system of dietary prohibitions. These are very prominent in primitive religions, yet in certain Protestant sects there is hardly any trace of them left. In the same way, sacrifice which, however, is characteristic of religions at a certain stage of development, has ended by losing all vitality of a truly ritual nature. Buddhism, Judaism and Islam[4] no longer practise sacrifice and in Christianity it survives only in a mythical and symbolic form. Prayer, on the contrary, which originally existed in an indefinite and rudimentary form with short and sparse formulae and chants of a magico-religious nature which could scarcely be called prayers, shows an uninterrupted line of development and ends by overrunning the whole ritual system. In liberal Protestantism, prayer has become practically the whole of religious life.[5] So prayer has been the remarkable tree which, having grown up in the shade of other trees, has ended by smothering them under its vast branches. The evolution of prayer is in part the evolution of religion itself; the progress made by prayer is similar to that made by religion.

Thus by tracing the development of prayer, it is possible to discern all the great trends which have influenced religious phenomena as a whole. It is known in fact, at least generally, that religion has undergone a double evolution. Firstly, it has become more and more spiritual. Whereas religion originally consisted of mechanical rites of a precise and material nature, of strictly formulated beliefs composed almost exclusively of tangible images, it has tended in the course of its history to give a greater place to consciousness. Rites have become attitudes of the soul rather than those of the body and have become enriched by mental elements, sentiments and ideas. Beliefs for their part become intellectualized and, growing less and less material and detailed, are being reduced to an ever smaller number of dogmas, rich and varied in meaning.[6] While becoming more spiritual, religion has tended to become increasingly individualistic. Rites began by being primarily collective in nature: they were almost always performed in common by the assembled group. At first, most beliefs existed only in a traditional form. Strictly obligatory, or at least communal, they were found throughout the group with a uniformity whose rigour is difficult for us to imagine today. Individual activity in relation to religious ideas and acts was exercised within the narrowest of limits. The evolution of religion has reversed the proportions and the final result is the limitation of group activity. For the most part religious practices have become truly individual. The time, place, conditions and form of any given act are less and less dependent on social causes. As individuals act more or less as they please, so they likewise become, so far as is possible, creators of their own faith. Some Protestant sects, the Remonstrants for example, attribute dogmatic authority to each member of the church. The 'interior God' of the most advanced religions is also the God of individuals.

These two processes are particularly marked in the case of prayer, which has in fact been one of the main agents of this double evolution. At first completely mechanical and effective only through the production of certain sounds, prayer finished by being completely mental and interior. Having at one time been only minimally cerebral, it has ended up by being no more than thought and an outpouring of the spirit. At first strictly collective, said in common or at least according to forms rigidly fixed by the religious group, sometimes even forbidden,[7] prayer becomes the domain of the individual's free converse with God. It is thanks to its oral nature that prayer has lent itself to this double transformation. Whilst manual rituals naturally tend to be modelled much more on the material effects to be produced than on the mental states from which they proceed, prayer, being speech, is thereby much closer to thought. That is why prayer was able to become abstract and spiritualized at the same time as religious things became more immaterial and transcendent. Besides, the words of which prayer is composed enjoy a relative mobility. More flexible than impersonal gestures, prayers have been able to follow the variations and nuances of individual consciousness, thus allowing the greatest possible scope for private initiative. So it is that prayer, while benefiting from religious evolution, has been at the same time one of the prime agents of that development.

One can see how very interesting is the whole question of prayer. Obviously one cannot study both the foundation and history of each and every manifestation of an institution so general and so complex. It is necessary to treat the problems and difficulties in order and to consider separately the various stages in a long process of development, as well as the multiple aspects and many functions of this fundamental ritual.

From what we have just said about the double interest to be found in the study of the origins of prayer and its evolution, it follows that a comprehensive study should comprise at least three parts.

In the first part we need to investigate primitive religions to see how prayer came into being. We would observe, if not its actual birth, at least its earliest infant cries. We would then seek its modest beginnings which may well be in the form of oral rites that may be richer and yet less refined than what we normally call 'prayers', that is, requests addressed to a divine or at least spiritual personality. In this way it is possible to reach, as far as possible, the shoots from which all the rest has sprung – shoots which may be as different from the first growth as a seed is different from the tree. Then we would study the first transformations of prayer, the first fixed and specific forms which it took. In order to do this, we would consider religions which are still close enough to the first religions we have studied and yet sufficiently evolved to have established a detailed prayer ritual. In this way the path is open to explain how prayer emerged from its rudimentary beginnings.

Once prayer proper has been established, along with a certain number of its principal divisions, it would become necessary to follow its evolution in the two directions indicated above. In order to discover the rules governing the progressive spiritualization of prayer, we need to find a type of religion with a long history. Here, starting with forms equivalent to those found in the most developed of the primitive religions just referred to, we would move up the scale without chronological or logical interruption to the highest and purest forms, to those which are most transformed to the spiritual. The society of ancient India provides the most favourable terrain to study here. In fact Vedic ritual certainly began in a form which calls to mind the most developed of Polynesian rituals. However, we know how far it progressed beyond that level. From the simple mantra of the Brahmin schools, whether from the central corpus of the Vedas or the Veda practised by magicians, there is an uninterrupted development within the same Vedic literature, to hymns which are mythic and moral, then philosophical and theosophical.[8] From there one goes on to mental prayer, to mystical concentration of thought, which is superior to any sort of rite and even superior to the gods. This is the *dhyâna* of the ascetic, which culminates either in the Buddhist Nirvana or in the annihilation of individual consciousness within the heart of the supreme brahman of the orthodox schools. Not only did these types of prayer logically succeed each other in the course of time, and not only is it possible to follow how one is regularly linked to the next, but also with each revolution of the religious institutions of India, they can be seen to co-exist in varying proportions. They constitute organic liturgies and harmonise with each other, enveloped within the compact body of beliefs and practices.

A third study will focus on the evolutionary process in which prayer increasingly becomes an individual rite. The typical example here is furnished primarily by the Semitic religions (of Syria and Palestine) and by the first centuries of the Christian religion. Whereas at a certain time, in most sanctuaries, the prayer of the simple devotee or lay person was so to speak forbidden, there came a time when it was expressly prescribed.[9] Prayer of a strictly liturgical and traditional type, said in common,[10] or by the priest, either in the name of the people or of the one offering sacrifice, was gradually supplanted, in many cases, by free prayer whose form was chosen by the faithful themselves, according to their own feelings and the circumstances. It even came about by a strange reversion that the ancient collective prayer, which was mechanical, of fixed wording and of obligation, became nothing more than one of the means of expression of the individual soul, and this on account of the poetic qualities that were attributed to prayer.

But the story of prayer is not one of uninterrupted ascent. There have also been regressions, which must be taken into account if we wish to trace the life history of this institution. Very often, prayers which were once wholly spiritual become simple recitations without any kind of personal content.[11] They sink to the level of a manual rite. One simply moves the lips rather than moving the limbs. Constantly repeated prayers, prayers in a language we do not understand, formulae which have lost all meaning,[12] whose words are so dated as to be incomprehensible, all these are striking examples of this type of regression. Furthermore, we sometimes see the most spiritual prayer degenerating to the point of becoming a mere material object: the rosary, the prayer-tree, the prayer-wheel, the amulet, phylacteries, *mezuzoth*, miraculous medals, scapulars, ex-votos,[13] are all truly materialized prayers. Prayer in religions whose dogmas have become detached from all fetishism, becomes itself a fetish.

Of these four parts, only the first is the subject of this book. The reason is that to understand the entire evolution of prayer, one must first start by knowing the elementary forms. We hope to proceed in an orderly fashion, according to the nature of the facts. The process is like that of the biologist who starts with the study of single-cell organisms and then can proceed to multi-cell organisms, sexed organisms and so on. We believe, in fact, that in sociology for a long time to come the study of elementary forms will be more interesting, more vital even to our understanding of contemporary forms, than the study of forms immediately preceding our own. It is not always the things nearest in time that are the profound causes of the facts with which we are acquainted. Thus the prayer systems of Greece and Rome, about which, moreover, there is little information,[14] and which seem to have been very meagre before what is called syncretism, have had but feeble influence on the system in Christian churches. Moreover, it is well-nigh impossible to follow any other order. The facts presented even by still barbarous rituals such as Vedic rituals, are so abundant and so involved that one would be at a loss to understand them, even with the help of such intelligent theologians as the Brahmins, if one did not possess the sort of guiding hypothesis that can only be derived from an analysis of primitive forms.

Chapter 2

I. A historical review

The paucity of scientific literature on a subject of such primordial importance is truly remarkable. Scholars, such as anthropologists and philologists who founded the science of religions, virtually never raised the problem.[15] For various reasons, it lay beyond the scope of their studies. The authors of the philological school, from Kuhn[16] and Max Müller[17] to V. Henry and Usener, asked no more of philology than it could give them. They made an objective analysis of the names of the gods and, either through those names or otherwise, of the myths that describe the gods. They sought to determine the meaning of the words uttered by the worshipper rather than to explain their efficacy. They scarcely went beyond the realm of belief.[18] Prayer, which is a rite, escaped their notice. As for the anthropologists, they were primarily concerned with discovering the common factors in the religious life of humankind in general and they scarcely studied advanced civilizations except to discover in them the traces of the most primitive civilizations.[19] That accounts for the weight they give to the study of survivals both in their own minds and in their various systems. So it is not surprising that they should have neglected prayer which, far from being a survival is, according to some of them, a late product of religious evolution.[20]

Historians were not able to show such a complete lack of interest. Either in manuals and dictionaries of the history of religion or in monographs (very rare, however), one can find excellent information about different rituals.[21] But historians are interested primarily in description. They search neither for principles nor laws. They describe the system of prayers in a particular religion. They study neither a type of prayer nor prayer in general. The links which they establish between facts are essentially, if not exclusively, chronological. They determine antecedents rather than causes. Without doubt these chronological links can be indicative of causal links. Sometimes it even happens when they deal with undated material, that it is on the basis of how facts condition each other hypothetically that the historians establish a chronological order. This is what has happened, above all in the case of the Vedic and Semitic ritual.[22] Thus the materials that we are researching have sometimes been worked on in a rudimentary way by historians. But such results have always been fragmentary, sporadic and accidental. Advantage will be taken of these initial explanations, which must be borne in mind. However, they do not constitute a theory.

Also, it must be added that historians have not always accorded our subject the interest it deserves. Ethnographers hardly mention it.[23] Historians of Eastern religions have shown a greater sense of its importance; but the extent of their work is scarcely commensurate with the place occupied by prayer in the religions they study. The Vedas, by which we mean the *samhitâs*, collections of hymns and verbal formulae, are nothing but a huge missal. Yet apart from Bergaigne's chapters on the subject,[24] there is probably no study of Vedic prayer viewed as a whole. The Vedas have been treated, quite rightly, as a collection of texts primarily to establish their history.[25] Their abundant facts were treated in the past primarily as a collection of myths, and today as a catalogue of rites of all kinds. Among these rites the main study has centred on magic and sacrifice rather than on prayer itself. It is only very recently that anyone has collated what the Brahmanas, the Brahminic commentaries on the Vedas, had to say about prayer.[26] Also, it is only recently that attention has been focussed on the curious figure of Brahmanaspati, the god of prayer who plays such an important role from the Vedas onwards and was destined to undergo such noble metamorphoses in the course of Indian history.[27] As for the other documents relating to Hindu liturgy, research has barely begun. The same applies to Buddhism, to Chinese religions and the Avestan gathas have served only to date the Avesta – and with what differences over dates! As for the religions of classical antiquity, historical literature on prayer is scarce, probably because there was little documentation. Only the Semitic and Christian religions differ to some extent in this respect. Practical requirements, the demands of exegesis, questions of ritual and theology, all these have given rise to studies of the history of Hebrew, Jewish and Christian liturgy, which are very important but still fragmentary.[28] It is difficult to discover the reason for this relative indifference as there is no lack of material. Thus, despite the number of εὔχαί in Greek literature and inscriptions, the history of this word has not yet been decided with precision, except on one point: the attitude of philosophers towards prayer.[29] It is only very recently that an intensive study has been made of the question of Assyro-Babylonian prayers[30] and incantations.[31] And yet liturgical cylinders make up nearly a quarter of all our written legacy of that civilization.[32] This is doubtless because historians in the past were quite satisfied with an external study of facts. Not long ago, history was still nothing more than a fairly fanciful recital of political events and of the most superficial events of social life. But the pressure of the developing social sciences has led historians to study social phenomena that are increasingly embedded in social life. Now prayer seems to be precisely one of the things that does not attract the attention of an observer who is scientifically meticulous but who lacks depth.

Until now, theologians and philosophers have been almost the only scholars who have considered prayer theoretically. But however interesting their theories, they are far from satisfying the demands of science.

Theologians have composed numerous theories of prayer. They have tried to discover why they prayed, why they used a certain prayer in certain circumstances. They have been led to classify and expound their prayers. Often their explanations,[33] discussions and classifications are extremely valuable because they sometimes had, in India for example, a very precise understanding of the rites which they practised.[34] But their own conception of these rites is not in itself anything more than a document describing their state of mind; however clear their religious consciousness may be, the account they give of their experiences is in no way scientific. They start with firm beliefs, accepted by their own religion, which they analyse in the course of writing them down as they go along, and it is with reference to these beliefs that they attempt to construct a more or less orderly system of their rites, ideas and feelings. Thus they sometimes see the facts in the light of religious ideas which in no way correspond to them, or do so no more. In this way an ancient practice is understood only in the light of a new dogma.[35] So a prayer which is purely magical, even theurgic, will appear in the theology of one of the rabbinical editors of the Talmud, or by a Father of the Church, as a prayer of adoration.[36] Finally one should not lose sight of the fact that theology has above all a practical purpose; its primary aim is to shape the liturgy. If theology tries to systematize and to understand prayers, it is above all with a view to propagating them or directing their use. So the historical research undertaken by theologians consists mainly in establishing which text is the most ancient, the most authentic, the most canonical, the most divinely inspired. This is the principle behind all theological speculations on prayer, from the treatise on the Berakôth in the Mishna and the Talmud, from the Didache and Irenaeus down to the countless number of Catholic, Orthodox, Protestant and Jewish works. For us these dogmatic theories are precious documents since they show how the most enlightened worshippers and often the authority of tradition itself, attached meaning to the various rites. But these are, properly speaking, mere facts.* They cannot do more than point in the direction of explanation. They are an aid to analysis and not a substitute for it.

The philosophers, for their part, attempted a rational explanation of prayer. They set out to discover its human origins. But they wanted to discover straightaway a general theory which would cover all the facts. They took for

---

* Facts, in the sense of phenomena for study. It is arguable that, in the writings of the Durkheimian school, *faits* is more naturally translated as 'phenomena' than 'facts'.

granted that there exists a single modality of religious sentiment which has manifested itself in prayer everywhere. For them, there is a religious mood common to all humanity and prayer is merely its expression; and they undertook to describe it. To achieve this, they considered that the most appropriate method was that of introspection. It seemed quite natural to them to analyse their own ideas, which were fully conscious and clearly understood – so they supposed – in order to understand the ideas of others. When they came to consider those intimate sentiments (*choses*) which were, so they thought, at the root of all things religious, they never thought to look elsewhere than in their own minds. But then it turns out that they are just like the theologians. What they are studying is not prayer but the idea that they have of prayer. And, as in the last analysis, one's ideas are always more or less a reflection of one's milieu, it is their own and their contemporaries' understanding of prayer that becomes the subject of study. From this point of view, their theories, like those of theologians, have no more than a documentary value. They no longer give us information about the practice itself but about the philosophers' conception of it or strictly what their contemporaries think of it. So the whole tenor of these discourses is dominated by the mental state of the authors. As they are defining nothing but their own ideas, they do not restrict themselves to the range of facts, which they would be obliged to cover completely, and which they would be forced to do, if they seriously wished to verify their conclusions. Philosophers are in no way obliged to take contradictory facts into consideration and there is nothing to prevent them from speculating on facts that more or less approximate to those they are studying but that are in reality profoundly different. Thus, even when they have been educated in the healthy school of the history of religions, they do little more than illustrate their own general opinions by examples, which may indeed be numerous and relevant but do not constitute proof. For the same reason the questions they discuss are not those imposed by the facts but those suggested by their personal preoccupations or those of the public. The terms in which they are expressed – the way in which they are drawn up – are not the necessary consequences of the method or of the natural relations of things, but result from subjective criteria, often even from current prejudices unconsciously shared by the author.

To clarify the ongoing observations, let us apply them to the theories of Tiele and Sabatier on prayer. We have chosen their theories because they are the most recent and also because of their very wide acceptance.

In a book which is a philosophy of the history of religions and religious institutions, Tiele[37] in the midst of a host of questions about worship, discusses prayer.[38] He sees it as a spiritual conversation with God, a movement towards the divinity. Accepting Christian doctrine[39] as it were *a priori*, he goes so far as to say that 'the response to God is prayer' and that this human act is itself the effect of a sort of reaction on God's part. So we are indeed in the presence of a completely subjective notion. The object under analysis is a personal state of mind peculiar to Tiele and his fellow-believers. What is more, when the author proceeds to deal with the philosophy of history and attempts to give a broad outline of the evolution of prayer, it is from this same subjective viewpoint that he examines and resolves problems which are however matters of fact. When he wishes to refute the theory that prayer originally had a coercive power over the god, and was originally theurgic,[40] he gives no more than a dialectical demonstration, relying on his own definition that prayer cannot come from magical incantation, 'in the same way that religion cannot come from superstition'. Thus it is his own idea of prayer and religion which dominates all his arguments. At the same time, it can be seen that the whole study concerns all the facts at once, with no set limits or preliminary division of any kind. He is dealing with the whole of prayer, all at once. There is also a lack of method in his research. Questions are chosen arbitrarily and many essential ones are overlooked; others, such as the universality of prayer, are rapidly settled although they are in fact insoluble.[41]

The same procedure and the same principles lead Sabatier to almost opposite conclusions. Tiele thought of prayer as an important but relatively secondary 'manifestation of religion'. For Sabatier, prayer is the essence of religion. 'Prayer,' he says, 'there you have religion in action'.[42]

As if every rite did not have this characteristic! As if the rite of touching a sacred object, like every contact with the divinity, were not equally a communication with God! Thus 'the inner bonding of the soul to the God who is within', such as takes place in the meditative prayer (*ἄρρητος ἄνωσις*) of an ultra-liberal Protestant, becomes the generic type of prayer, the essential act of every religion. That is, religion and prayer are defined by their most advanced forms, which are the most subtle and rare. Sabatier, it is true, is the first to recognize that his views are the result of an evolutionary process and he undertakes to trace this evolution for us.[43] So he shows how, in the beginning, the only religious element in prayer was the belief in its efficacy. Unlike Tiele, he admits that primitive prayer held the gods in thrall. Then, according to him, fetishism and polytheism established a sort of contract between the gods and humans who, thenceforward, prayed in order to receive things. The religion of Israel made a further step forward: piety and morality were combined and the result was a prayer of trust, abandonment and joy. But the fierce monotheism of Judaism left human beings in fear of a God who was too distant from them. With the advent of the Gospel comes the full development of prayer and since Jesus' time, human beings have been able to address God as Father.[44] But however interesting this historical account may be, one can see how arbitrarily the facts have been selected. On the origins of prayer and fetishism (supposing that it existed), on the Mosaic tradition and Christianity, all we are given are cursory opinions and philosophical short-cuts which cannot be regarded as proving anything. It is impossible to express the essence of great religions in a few lines, however skilfully condensed. Moreover, there is no examination of some essential facts which would invalidate the theory. Thus Sabatier takes it for granted that prayer is an individual phenomenon (*fait*), while in many religions it is forbidden for the lay person or for women to pray.[45] In fact, the outcome of the discussion is predetermined by the faith of the author. It is much less a question of analysing the facts than of demonstrating the superiority of the Christian religion.

II. Prayer as a social phenomenon

If the theorists have confined themselves to generalities, it is because in presenting the problem as they did, they ignored the data necessary to solve it. In fact for them prayer is an essentially individual phenomenon. It is something that takes place in the inmost heart – an activity of the spiritual person, a manifestation of the individual's state of soul.[46] As for the forms it takes, they see in them a sort of degradation.* According to these theorists, prayer becomes something external and artificial, a sort of language which an ecclesiastical authority or some poet or specialist has invented for the convenience of the faithful, something which takes on meaning only by virtue of the personal sentiments which it expresses. Under these conditions, prayer becomes an elusive phenomenon which can only be understood by self-questioning or by questioning those who pray. The one possible method is introspection, combined with the check on speculation afforded by the introspection of others – the 'religious experiences' as they are called, which have been recorded in theological literature. Therefore, whether one engages in personal introspection or has recourse to related psychological statistics which are so fashionable nowadays, one can determine by such methods only how a certain number of individuals imagine that they pray. But we are always performing actions whose rationale, meaning, scope and true nature elude us: often our efforts at bringing them to consciousness end only in self-deception. The conception we can form of even a habitual action is no more than a totally inadequate expression of that action. It is one thing to have an empirical knowledge of a language, even that of a poet or dramatist, quite another to have the knowledge of a philologist or linguist. In the same way, prayer is one thing and one's own unaided representation of it, even if one is religious and cultivated, is quite another.

If there is one subject for which introspective observation is totally inadequate, that subject is certainly prayer. Far from being the product of individual consciousness alone, and therefore easily understood by means of

---

* French *chute* literally means 'fall', and it may here connote the Christian doctrine of the Fall of Man. The theorists Mauss is criticizing lack awareness of the social dimension of religion.

introspection, prayer is full of all sorts of elements whose origin and nature escape us. Every myth and rite converge in prayer. For example, let us analyse one of the simplest religious formulae,[47] that of the blessing: *In nomine patris*, etc. Nearly the whole of Christian dogma and liturgy can be found closely entwined in this formula. *In nomine*: here is the virtue attributed to the very word of blessing, in the name of God, and special virtue is attached to the person who pronounces the formula, which implies the whole priestly organization when it is a priest who blesses, and the laicisation (*individualisation*) of religion when it is a layperson who blesses, etc. *Patris*: the name of father given to a unique god, which leads to monotheism and the conception of the interior god, etc. *Filii*: the dogma of the son, Jesus, Messianism, the sacrifice of the god, etc. *Spiritus sancti*: the dogma of the Spirit, the Logos, the Trinity, etc. Above all, prayer as a whole bears the marks of the Church in her role as organizer of dogma and ritual. And even today we are not yet able to understand the full import of such an apparently simple utterance. It is complex, not only on account of its numerous components, but also because each of them is the product of a long history which naturally cannot be seen by the individual mind. An invocation, such as the beginning of the Lord's Prayer, is the fruit of the work of centuries. A prayer is not just the effusion of a soul, a cry which expresses a feeling. It is a fragment of a religion. In it one can hear the echo of numberless phrases; it is a tiny piece of literature, it is the product of the accumulated efforts of men and women over generations.

What we are saying is that prayer is beyond doubt a social phenomenon because the social character of religion is now sufficiently well established. A religion is an organic system of collective ideas and practices relating to acknowledged sacred beings. Even when prayer is individual and free, even when the worshippers choose freely the time and mode of expression, what they say always uses hallowed language and deals with hallowed things, that is, ones endorsed by social tradition. Even in mental prayer where, according to the formula, Christians abandon themselves to the Spirit, ἀναχρατη θῆναι τῳ πνεύματι, this spirit which controls them is the spirit of the Church. The ideas they generate are those of the teaching of their own sect and the sentiments which they speculate on are in accord with the moral doctrine of their denomination. Buddhists, in their ascetic meditation, exercises and *karmasthâna*, will deliberate among themselves quite otherwise because their prayer is the expression of a different religion.

Prayer is social not only in content but also in form. Its forms are exclusively social in origin. It does not exist apart from some kind of ritual. We do not take the case of the formal systems of primitives where it would be all too easy to argue the case. Even in the highest religions, those which call everyone to use the same prayer, most of the faithful use only the established prayer books. The *tephilah* and the *mahzor*, the liturgical suras, the prayer book and the breviary, the *Book of Common Prayer* and the prayer books of the various denominations, amply satisfy the needs of the great majority of believers. Not only is the text traditional but it takes concrete form in a book – in *the book*. From another angle, the circumstances, time and place where the prayer should be said, the required posture, all these are strictly laid down. So even in the religions which allow most scope to the individual, all prayer is a ritual form of speech adopted by a religious society.[48] It is a series of words whose meaning is determined, and whose order is approved as orthodox by the group.[49] Its value is that given to it by the community. It is efficacious because the religion declares it to be so. Doubtless in certain religions the individual can sometimes pray without adhering to forms imposed from without. But this is rare and interior meditation has not become a normal practice. What is more, however freely one prays, one always observes the general principles of ritual simply by not violating those principles. Consciously or not, one conforms to certain norms and adopts an approved attitude.[50] And it is with the language of ritual that the internal discourse is composed. So individuals are merely adapting to their personal feelings a language which they did not invent. Ritual remains the very foundation of the most individual of prayers.

Prayer clearly can be shown to be essentially a social phenomenon in religions where it is said only by the group or by priestly authority. There even exists a precise rule *forbidding* any other way of praying. That is the case in India. Anyone who is not a Brahmin is *forbidden* to pray.[51] Brahmins, according to the meaning of the word Brahmin, are those who do pray.[52] They are the men of *brahman*, the sacred word. They share this function with no one else. This is all the more remarkable because communal sacrifice, and in general all the popular ceremonies of a national or urban nature, *seem* to have disappeared from Brahminism properly so-called. It is always for an individual and not for the group that the rites are performed.[53] But the beneficiary is not the author of the rites: he is not permitted to perform them and consequently he may not recite the prayers if he himself is not a priest. At the very least, if he is allowed to take some part in the religious act, it is only at the invitation of the priest and according to a strictly prescribed form. He merely repeats the *mantra*, which he is made to recite. And this is the prerogative only of higher castes: the *kshatriyas*, nobles and freemen, initiates, those who have received the sacred thread. Although they also are 'twice-born', they pray only through the intermediary of someone to whom the religious group has given the right and exclusive power of prayer. As for the lower castes, the great gods regard them with horror and pay no attention to their prayers.

With the Jews, there is no explicit prohibition of individual prayer. But in fact the only written prayers we have are essentially communal.[54] These are, in the first place, canticles sung either by the whole congregation[55] or by the groups of pilgrims going up to Jerusalem, or by the community of the righteous and poor, where a large number of the chants were composed.[56] Then there are liturgical Psalms, obviously intended to be recited in public.[57] The form in which most of them are written actually betrays their Levitical and priestly character: either they have a rubric which determines their use in the temple services,[58] or else they are worded in a way which shows that they were recited by groups of singers.[59] A third group consists of clearly popular songs which were taken to be religious chants once the Hebrew and the original meaning were no longer understood.[60] Lastly comes a collection of imitations of ancient models. Even the most recent texts, such as the prayer of Solomon,[61] speak above all of the prayer of a whole people. Finally, we recall the evolution of Judaism in the long conflict between the Temple and the Synagogue, and the great difficulty in forming the prayer of the Synagogue before it became accepted as legitimate, despite the fact that it was still congregational in form. This clearly shows that at the start, prayer was confined to the Temple, to its congregation, and to the Levites who represented the Temple – one division to each tribe – also to the worshippers who came, accompanied by the priests, to approach Yahweh and fulfil their vows or make expiation.[62]

Admittedly, these are only two particular cases, that of *a single* temple and that of a *single* religion[63] and they may be due to the control exercised over the forms of worship by the two types of priesthood. But at the very least, these two examples prove that prayer *can* only be a social phenomenon. In any case, the underlying causes of such a development run deep. As we shall see, this can be observed in primitive religions. In the beginning, only prayers that are communal or have a strictly communal form are to be found.[64] Certainly there is no evidence that individual prayer was officially forbidden. But at first, as primitive ritual was not codified into precise rules, one cannot expect to find a prohibition of such a kind. What is more, the absence of such a prohibition may well be due to the fact that the idea of individual prayer simply did not even exist. In any case, whatever the truth of the matter, the very fact that in two important and significant cases prayer appears to be essentially a social phenomenon, justifies the conclusion that it is not essentially an individual phenomenon.

The final proof that prayer is a collective phenomenon lies in its relation to other collective phenomena. More particularly, there is a whole group of activities, obviously social, that are closely related to prayer. These are legal and moral formulae.[65] A theory of prayer will certainly be of help to anyone wishing to understand the oath, the solemn contract,[66] the turns of phrase required by etiquette, whether in the context of leaders, kings, law courts or parliaments, or indeed, the language of common courtesy. All these things are so closely related to prayer that later on we shall have to consider how they differ from it. The opening words of most of the sacramental prayers in Catholicism and the opening words of our legal judgments are the same, almost word for word. The ritual expressions, as *In nomine Patris*, etc. correspond to the hallowed words 'In the name of the French people, etc.'. Both of them have evocative value and place the thing solemnized under the protection of a being which they both name and make present. And in a general way, it is by its formulae that prayer is bound to the whole concept of formalism.[67] Consequently, prayer helps us to understand formalism. Even the creative character of the forms imposed by society is nowhere more evident than in prayer. Their virtue *sui generis*, the distinctive stamp they give to actions, is seen more clearly in prayer than in any other institution. For prayer acts only through the word and the word is the most formal thing there is. Therefore the efficacious power of form is never as evident as it is in prayer. Creation by the word is the very type of creation *ex nihilo*.[68]

It is even true to say that there is hardly any sphere of social life where prayer does not, or has not played some part. It bears on family organization at initiation, and in marriage etc. It cements a union or an adoption. It comes into all kinds of legal situations in the form of the oath.[69] It is linked with morals in confession, expiatory prayer, the avowal of guilt. It even has economic functions. In fact prayers are often real assets,[70] they contribute to the wealth of priestly classes. What is more, there are whole civilizations where prayers are thought to aid productivity. The efficacy attributed to them is similar to that of work or of mechanical skills. For many Australian tribes, the best way to ensure the reproduction of the animal species they eat is to perform certain ceremonies, to say certain words, to recite certain chants.

But when we say that prayer is a social phenomenon, we do not mean that it is in no way an individual phenomenon. That would be a misunderstanding of our thesis. We do not think that society, religion and prayer are extraordinary things, that is, are conceivable without the individuals who live within them. But we do believe that, while it takes place in the mind of the individual, prayer is above all a social reality outside the individual and in the sphere of ritual and religious convention. In fact, we are merely reversing the order in which the two terms are usually studied: we are discounting neither of them. Instead of seeing in individual prayer the principle behind collective prayer, we are making the latter the principle behind the former. Thus we avoid the error of deriving the complex from the simple – the canonical prayer of the Church from the spontaneous prayer of the individual. But that does not mean that we fail to realize the importance of the individual element. We do not know whether individuals were permitted or were able to pray in their own way from the beginning; there is no proof of this and it would be difficult to find a convincing one. We shall however find that inventors of prayer have existed from the beginning. But the role necessarily played by the individual in taking part in collective practices, does not detract from their collective character. As each person, when speaking a national language, has an individual style and accent, so each person can create a personal prayer without prayer ceasing to be a social institution. As for those prayers which are composed by individuals and become part of a ritual, from the moment they are incorporated in the ritual, they cease to be individual. Moreover, if they have been deemed suitable for general use and become obligatory, it is firstly because they met the requirements of an established ritual and secondly, because they met the needs of religious innovation for the group. Finally, they also owe their success to the authority which public opinion confers on their authors. These were not just ordinary poets but priests, prophets, seers, that is, people whom the community believes to be in contact with the gods.[71] When they speak, it is the gods who speak through them. They are not mere individuals: they are themselves social forces.

III. Method

We have now to determine the best method to treat the subject. Although we are not in favour of constant discussions of methodology,[72] it would nevertheless seem helpful at this point to explain the procedures of definition, observation and analysis which will be used in the course of this work. It will enable the reader to assess each step of our argument and to check the results.

Once prayer, as an integral part of a ritual, is recognised as a social institution, the study has a subject matter, an object, a thing with which it can and should deal. In fact, whilst for philosophers and theologians, ritual is a conventional language which imperfectly expresses the play of intimate images and sentiments, it becomes, for us, reality itself. For it contains everything which is active and living in prayer. It keeps in reserve all the meaning put into the words and it holds in embryo everything that can be deduced from it, even by means of new syntheses. The social practices and beliefs which appear in it in condensed form are laden with the past and present and are pregnant with the future. So, when one studies prayer from this angle, it ceases to be something inexpressible and inaccessible. It becomes a clearly defined reality, a concrete fact, something precise, resistant and fixed which imposes itself on the observer.

Definition – Although we now know that somewhere there exists a system of facts called 'prayers', we still have only a confused understanding of it. We do not know its extent or exact limits. It is necessary, at the outset, to change this vague and imprecise impression into a clear picture. That is the purpose of definition. There is no question, of course, of defining the very substance of the facts straight away. Such a definition can come only at the end of our study: the one we must make at the beginning can only be provisional. It is meant simply to stimulate research, to determine the object of our study, without anticipating its results. We need to know what things deserve to be called prayers. But, despite its provisional nature, all care must be taken to establish this definition because it will govern all the rest of the work. In fact, it facilitates research because it limits the field of observation. At the same time it enables us to make a methodical examination of hypotheses. Thanks to it, arbitrary steps in the argument can be avoided and one is obliged to consider all the facts relating to prayer and nothing else. This means that a critical appraisal can be made following precise rules. In order to question a proposition one must demonstrate either that the definition was faulty and so invalidated all the subsequent argument, or that some fact relating to the definition had been overlooked, or finally, that facts had been taken into account which were not covered by the definition.

Otherwise, when there is no fixed terminology, the author passes imperceptibly from one order of facts to another, or the same order of facts goes under different names with different authors. The disadvantages arising from an absence of definition are particularly obvious in the science of religions, a field in which little care has been taken to define accurately. Thus, it happens that ethnographers, having asserted that prayer is unknown in some society or other, then go on to mention 'religious chants' and numerous ritual texts that they have observed.[73] A preliminary definition would spare us this deplorable vagueness and those endless debates between authors, who under the same heading, do not talk about the same things.

Since this definition comes at the start of the research, that is, at a time when the facts are known only from the outside, it can only be made according to outward signs. It is merely a question of narrowing down the field of study and thereby establishing its outlines. We need to find a few obvious and easily perceptible features which allow us to recognize almost at first sight anything that can be called 'prayer'. But on the other hand these same features must be objective. We cannot rely on our own impressions or preconceptions, nor on those of the group under observation. We do not say that a religious act is a prayer because we feel it is, or because the worshippers in some religion or other call it so.[74] Just as a physicist defines heat by the expansion of solids and not by the mere impression of heat, so it will be in the external world itself that we shall seek the basis for our preliminary formulation of what counts as prayer. To define a word according to one's impressions means not to define it at all, since nothing is as unstable as an impression. It can change from one individual to another, from one people to another. It can change in an individual as in a people according to the prevailing mood. Thus, when instead of establishing the scientific notion of prayer – arbitrarily, we admit, but with a view to logic and a sense of the concrete –we knit together their notions of prayer using such inconsistent elements as the feelings of individuals, then we see the process tossed about between meanings that are absolutely incompatible and are detrimental to our work. The most diverse things are called 'prayers', sometimes in the course of a single work by the one author, sometimes by different authors giving different meanings to the word, and sometimes according to the civilizations being studied.[75] In this way, it happens that things which belong to the same category are presented as contradictory, or things which should be seen as different are in fact placed together. In the same way as ancient physics saw heat and cold as having two separate natures, so even today an idealist will refuse to admit that there is any kinship between prayer and crude magical incantation. The only way to avoid inappropriate distinctions or equally arbitrary confusions, is to eliminate, once and for all, all subjective preconceptions, in order to reach the institution itself. If it does this, the initial definition will already be one step forward in our research. For, the property the definition emphasises is an objective one and therefore goes some way towards expressing the nature of what is defined. Although the definition is external, it is solidly bound up with the more essential properties, thus making these easier to discover. In the same way, the expansion of bodies, by which heat is [initially] defined, corresponds to the molecular movements discovered by thermodynamics.

Observation – Once the facts have been defined, we must encounter with them, that is, we must observe them. But observation with regard to our subject presents special difficulties and is carried out under special conditions. The facts which provide material for a theory of prayer are not immediately apparent, as an organism is to a zoologist who is describing it. They are recorded in historical or ethnographical documents which have to be examined in such a way as to determine their true nature. A special procedure is thus necessary in order to pick them out and, to some extent, construct them. Criticism is the name given by the historical sciences to this particular method of observation. Starting from the same data as history, sociology must apply the identical methods to them. No doubt criticism arose outside sociology but it must incorporate the same essential principles because it can do nothing with inauthentic or imaginary facts. Here is something which has all too often been forgotten in ethnography. There are no facts in this field that stand in more urgent need of criticism and none to which it has been so little applied.[76] Even the anthropological school ordinarily employs ethnographic material without subjecting it to sufficient criticism.[77]*

But it is not enough to say that sociology should borrow its methods from history. While sociology makes general use of historical methods, it does so in a different spirit. It makes them clearer, more explicit, more rigorous: it extends their sphere of application while keeping them in their place. For it is a fact that historians have almost made criticism the aim of their research. Laying down as a principle that a fact cannot be used before it has been established in every detail, they waste endless time in hopeless discussions and keep putting off the moment of systematization. If, on the contrary, one regards criticism as a simple initial scientific tool, it can be directed towards clearly defined goals.

* Mauss is referring to Anglophone ethnology and probably more particularly to British or British-influenced ethnology.

The first thing to be done with a document is to discover its value,[78] that is, to establish how much error it contains, taking into account its present condition, the means whereby it has come down to us, its date, its sources, etc. This is usually called external criticism. Naturally, we shall have to use it in different ways, according to whether we are dealing with texts or with indirect information concerning prayer. Take some examples from the field of ethnography because it is this area which will mainly concern us in the next part [Book II] of this opening study. If, until now, ethnographical information has been too much scorned by certain sociologists, it is simply because they had not subjected it to the necessary criticism. In fact it is quite possible to determine the part played by personal interpretation in any given observation. Thus when an anthropologist, even one as discriminating as Curr, tells us that the Australians have no prayers, we shall not lend any credence whatever to his statement. Firstly, because he is given to hasty negations of this sort. Secondly, because he himself gives us an account of a certain number of rites which indeed deserve to be called prayers.[79] When we have before us genuine prayer texts, we are nearer to the original facts, but we still need to take into consideration everything which separates us from those facts. Generally we have nothing but translations whose value must be determined according to the competence and conscientiousness of the author etc. Then we have to assess the authenticity of the document in question, according to the conditions under which it was acquired, the informant who dictated it, etc. Thus Ellis in his *Polynesian Researches*[80] gives a long text of a hymn without mentioning in which part of Tahiti he observed it, at which period, and where it originated. In addition we know that although Ellis had a very good knowledge of the island's language, he was also a very religious person. So we should use this text only with due caution – necessary both because of the uncertainties that surround the text and because of the prejudices of the translator.

But not only must we criticize the document itself but also the fact reported by the document. To have carried out the first task does not absolve us from performing the second even when the document is dated. This is because, for example, a recent document can record ancient facts, and of two documents of different dates, it is not always in the more recent that the more up-to-date facts are to be found. Thus in the Bible we find rites which are obviously more recent than certain magical rites which are preserved only in the Talmud. This second type of criticism has been called 'internal criticism'. Its aim is to establish the fact itself, situating it in its milieu and breaking it down into its component parts. To this end, the date is determined, that is basically the religious period and ritual system to which it belongs, the significance that it has as a whole and in each of its parts. In order to determine all this, historians employ various procedures which all seem to us to be based on the same obviously sociological principle, namely, the interdependence of social phenomena. For example, a prayer is dated according to the antiquity of the verbal and syntactic forms it uses, which really amounts to relating the two social institutions of prayer and language.[81] Or maybe it is shown that a certain text mentions or presupposes events which could have happened only at a given point of evolution. Or again, a series of hymns is classified chronologically on the principle that 'pure forms' depend on 'impure forms' and consequently are later, or vice versa. However, generally speaking, it is easy to understand how all these arguments are based on the same fundamental axiom: how can one link something to a certain background unless one shows how that background has influenced the thing in question?

This being the assumption of internal criticism, the historians who use this method are, whether consciously or not, acting as sociologists.[82] Now the application of a method tends to be more regular and more reliable the more it is used consciously. So when the sociologist adopts the methods of criticism he cannot fail to make more fruitful use of them.

Once the basic principle of the critical method has thus become clear, one is better able to apply it in accordance with its true nature.

In particular, one is less liable to substitute other principles which have neither the same meaning nor value. Thus criticism, and above all Biblical criticism, has sometimes made bad use of the principle of contradiction. It is taken as evident that two contradictory or merely opposite things are necessarily of different date or origin. For example, according to most authors,[83] the *dânastuti* (praises and blessings called down on the one making the sacrifice) which come at the end of a large number of Vedic hymns, are interpolations, simply because they do not immediately fit in with the rest of the text. But it was never necessary that they should have been intimately linked. To assume that prayers are all of necessity well composed is to misunderstand the true nature of the links by which social phenomena are joined together. If there is one thing that the science of religions has brought to light, it is that a single religious idea or even a single religious act can have extremely different, even contradictory meanings. The one social institution can have the most varied functions and produce the most opposite effects. The one prayer can begin quite unselfishly and end selfishly. A simple logical contradiction is far from being a sign of a veritaable incompatibility between the facts.

At the same time one gets rid of a certain number of more or less idle questions, dear to the practitioners of criticism, and one is led to ask more essential ones. It is often assumed that each prayer is the work of one author and, in order to establish the text and its meaning, it is asked: who was this author? How did he express himself? What were his ideas? Posed in those terms the question is usually unanswerable. In fact religions generally attribute the composition of prayers to mythical authors, gods, heroes or seers. But even where prayers have been truly invented by individuals, as in recent religions, ritual has shown a certain tendency to eliminate all trace of individual particularities. If one regards prayer as a social institution,[84] the real, critical question is quite different. From then on the essential question is no longer which author composed that prayer, but which group used it, under what conditions and at what stage of religious evolution? We no longer look for the original text but for the received text, that is, the one that is traditional and canonical. We cease to examine the words in order to find one person's ideas, but those of a group of people.

From this same point of view, the problem of the date becomes much less weighty. Of course, questions of chronology cannot be neglected. But, having said that, the value of any given element for a systematic theory of prayer depends much less on its approximate age than on the place which it occupies in the general body of ritual. The most important task is to situate it, not in time but in the liturgy. Take for example the collection of Psalms known as the Hallel. Its date is uncertain but it is easier to determine its use in the ritual. We can establish that these Psalms were chanted at the sacrifices at the three great feasts and at the New Moon but not on the Sabbath, at Rosh Hashanah or at Yom Kippur.[85] This means that they were part of the ritual of the ancient, solemn sacrifices. Their significance is thus fully established which makes it easier to insert them either in a theory of Jewish prayer or of prayer in general. And in addition, the question of the date is clarified to some extent. For the Hallel is thus attached to the most ancient of the temple liturgies, those of the agrarian and astronomical feasts, as distinct from those of the Sabbath and the Mosaic feasts. Therefore we would hesitate to say that no Psalms of this type existed at the time of the first Temple, without however being able to affirm that the present collection of Psalms was then in use.

So the task of the sociologist is no less demanding than that of the most conscientious historian. He, too, strives to see the facts in all their detail and makes a point of relating them to a well described context. But the attachment to detail is not for him the whole of his discipline and the context to which his attention is directed is primarily the whole range of social institutions within which any one fact takes its place. Conducted in this way, criticism is in no danger of getting lost in commentaries and discussions aroused by mere curiosity. Instead, it prepares the way for explanation.

Explanation. To explain is to establish a rational order between the facts, once they have been ascertained. The sociologist who deals with prayer must not in fact confine himself to describing methods of prayer in one society or another. He has to investigate the relations that link the facts of prayer, both to each other and to other facts that condition them. It is a matter of constructing a hierarchy of mutually illuminating ideas, which taken as a whole constitutes a theory of prayer.

But such a systematization can operate in two different ways. Firstly, one can form a generic idea by analysing a greater or lesser number of phenomena, which have been selected with adequate care. This is expressed in a formula which provides the schema, as it were, of the phenomenon to be explained, whether it is prayer or sacrifice, punishment, or the family. One can then seek to discover the very general characteristics of the facts whose analysis led to the generic idea. Having done this one examines how the schematic formula varies, when such and such a factor is introduced which makes the institution itself vary. In this manner one has a system of concepts proceeding from the most general to the most particular, in which can be seen why and when the genus, enriched by different specifics, gives rise to a diversity of species. This is the method that we ourselves have used on another occasion.[86]

But there is a second explanatory procedure which may equally well be employed. Instead of starting from the genus in order to finish with the species, we start from the most rudimentary forms presented by the phenomenon under consideration in order to pass progressively to the most developed forms and we show how the latter have evolved from the former. Thus we have, with the first method, a hierarchical series of ideas. Only, however, in the schematic explanation, the analysist stands outside time and space, since he considers the genus and all the species as if they were present at one and the same logical moment. Here, on the contrary, we are dealing with types which have actually succeeded each other in time and which have given rise to one another and the aim is to retrace the order in which they arose. That is why this sort of explanation can be called genetic. Thus, as far as our subject is concerned, if we use the first procedure, we shall start by accurate observation which will help us to determine the constitutive characteristics of prayer in general. Then we shall proceed to discover how and in what circumstances prayer becomes expiation, thanksgiving, a hymn, petition, votive prayer etc. If we explain prayer genetically, we ask what is the most rudimentary of all known forms of prayer. We then determine the immediately superior form which developed from it and the way in which it did so, and we continue in the same manner, until we reach the most recent forms. In India, for example, we shall see certain Vedic hymns expressing a syncretical pantheism, which give birth to the mystical prayer[87] of the Upanishads, while this in turn leads on to ascetic meditation of the Brahminic or Buddhist types.

Although the two methods are equally valid, the second seems more suited to the study of prayer. In fact when it is a question of an institution that has developed constantly and that in the course of this development has taken on a multiplicity of forms, the schematic explanation cannot give a true picture of the facts because it is not historically based. It is not really suitable except when a phenomenon somewhere assumes sufficiently definite forms that enable us to abstract its essence with relative ease, and when also the number and importance of the variations it has undergone are sufficiently limited. Now prayer, as we have seen, is in a constant state of development. It would be very difficult to fix a moment at which it is more fully realized than at any other time. So the historical succession of forms becomes the important factor in the explanation.

Besides, in a general way, genetic explanation presents certain advantages. It follows the order of phenomena and so leaves less room for error. By this very fact it makes omissions harder because just one lacuna in the course of the development would create a break in continuity that would be quickly felt. Moreover, it is easier to get a clear idea of the nature of the facts when one looks at their genesis. Finally, a genetic explanation can help prepare the ground for a schematic explanation, which will be greatly enhanced by coming after a methodical review and initial systematization of the facts.

The first step in a genetic explanation is to establish a genealogical classification of the types of prayer, that is to say, to organize the types by arranging them in the order of their evolution. As this sort of classification proceeds, it provides in itself a preliminary explanation. In fact the raw material for each type of prayer is provided by the type or types immediately preceding it, so its genealogy tells us its basic content. But by deriving the superior form from the inferior in this way, we have no intention of explaining the complex by means of the simple. For the most rudimentary forms are in no way simpler than the most developed forms. Their complexity is merely of a different sort.[88] The elements, which will become conspicuous and be modified in the course of further evolution, are all present together at the start, but in a state of mutual penetration. Their unity results from their confusion, which is such that the type cannot be characterized by any of them, but rather by a sort of mixture or fusion. This conflation or interfusion is so intimate that any radical separation of the elements would be arbitrary and contrary both to reason and the facts of the case. We must be on our guard against the all too common mistake of the conception of primitive forms as being reduced to a single element. All sorts of insuperable difficulties have arisen from this initial error. Thus people still sometimes argue about whether prayer originates from magical incantation or vice versa.[89] In reality, if we are to derive it from anything, it will be from a more complex principle that includes both prayer and magic.

But if the more organised forms arise from the more rudimentary ones, these latter do not contain the cause of their development within themselves. Genealogical classification gives us a well reasoned picture of origins, but it does not in fact show us the determining factors. The forces which transform the system of prayer are necessarily exterior to it. Where then can they be found? We shall not find them in the mental make-up of the individual. The general laws of human representation, which are the same everywhere, cannot explain such a diversity of types. The most they can do is to account for the possibility of prayer in general. In any case, such an explanation, which relies on the most remote conditions, is obviously far removed from the actual facts. Even less could it help us to understand why a certain religion has a particular system of prayers and why, for example, mystical prayer has developed in one case whereas the prayer of adoration has developed in another. The true determining factors immediately related to all these variations cannot be found except in a milieu that is equally variable and has directs links with prayer. This is the social milieu. There is a necessary link between a given prayer, a given society and a given religion. And right away we can say that certain types of prayer are characteristic of particular types of social organization and vice-versa. Thus, when we find magico-religious prayers for the maintenance of certain animal or vegetable species, we can be sure that we are dealing with totemic groups.[90] This determining character of social causes can also be seen in the diversity of transformations sometimes undergone by the same type of prayer according to the milieux in which it develops. From the same Buddhist ritual, essentially meditative and spiritual to begin with, have emerged forms as diverse as the *dharani* of Tibet, Japan, Nepal or China, which is a real materialization of prayer, and the mystical formulae of the Siamese and Burmese [Buddhist] priests. Similarly, Catholicism and Orthodoxy have developed a mechanical and idolatrous sort of prayer whilst Protestantism developed a mental and interior type of prayer. This is because the one form contains within itself possibilities that are very varied and may even be opposed to each other, and one or other of these possibilities will be realized according to the circumstances. This shows, as well, that the evolution of prayer is not subject to a rigid determinism but on the contrary, leaves room for contingency.

As for the instrument of genetic explanation, it is the same whether it is a question of genealogical classification or the discovery of causes. It is the comparative method. For, when dealing with social phenomena, we cannot make any sort of explanation except by way of comparison.

First of all, the establishment of types obviously implies that we have brought together different systems of prayers in order to define their common characteristics. But care must be taken to compare only those things that are truly comparable. So the different rituals that are to form one type must belong to religions of the same order. It is true that, at the present stage of research in the subject, we cannot rely on an objective classification of religions. However it is undeniable that even at the present time, broad categories are beginning to be established, so we can limit the field of comparison in such a way as to avoid collating facts that are too discordant. For example, no one will question our right to compare Australian religions one with another and thus to determine the nature of prayer in religions of the same type. In such comparisons it is above all the similarities that are significant. However, if we do not at the same time look very carefully for the differences, we run the risk of mistaking wholly fortuitous resemblances for essential ones, for the most dissimilar things can be alike in some ways and so be classified together. In the same way as every animal that lives in water has been defined as a fish, so one could define the hymn by the fact that it is sung and go on to confuse it with popular songs. On the other hand, these superficial similarities always bring with them equally superficial differences and thus can lead one to posit radical contrasts between things that are of the same nature. Just because the hymn has been linked with song, one could separate it from prayer, of which it is simply a variety. If we seem to insist on this rule of method, it is because it has been too often overlooked in the science of religions and, more generally, in sociology. As our discipline is only in its early stages, our attention is more readily given to the similarities which are striking because of their repetition. There is a failure to extend the analysis as far as the elements which differ. In this way, scholars have formed huge but ill-defined classes of facts, composed of elements that are basically heterogeneous. This is the case with current ideas relating to totemism, taboo, the cult of the dead, patriarchy, matriarchy, etc.

Once the types have been established, their genealogy becomes apparent almost of its own accord. The higher type is always as it were rooted in the lower type immediately preceding it. They have common elements which reveal their kinship. In fact, in most cases, the elementary forms do not entirely disappear before the higher forms[91] but they persist underneath, beside or even within the latter, as if to witness to their origin. So in India we see the simple magical *mantra* persisting side by side with ascetic prayer.[92] Moreover, it often happens that we can follow directly in history the evolution in the course of which new types have come into being; and then it is no longer necessary to work out the order in which they appeared, one needs only to observe it.

In order to establish types, the comparison bears immediately on similarities, but when we wish to determine causes, it is the differences which prove more instructive. Thus, the distinctive characteristics of Australian prayer which form the starting-point of our research, depend on the specific characteristics of the Australian social milieu. So it is by bringing together the differential features of this social organization and those of this sort of prayer that we can discover the causes of the latter. Such a method is all the more suitable when, having passed beyond the elementary forms, we have to carry out research on how prayer has evolved. This is because the successive changes the forms have undergone are obviously related to the parallel changes which have taken place in the corresponding social milieux.

But in these social milieux we can distinguish as it were two concentric spheres, one made up of all the general institutions of the society, the other of all the religious institutions. These two factors play an obviously unequal part in the formation of types of prayers. Sometimes the social organization, whether it be political, legal or economic, acts directly. For example, there may be prayers belonging to the national cult, or the household cult, prayers for hunting or fishing etc. Even the structure of prayer often depends on the social structure. Thus, the elementary forms of prayer will appear to be linked to the organization of the clan. However, in general, prayer is more immediately related to other religious phenomena and it is under their direct action that it evolves. So prayer is quite different according to whether mythical powers are personified or not, and whether there is a priesthood or not. Of course, even in these last cases, it is still the general social milieu that is the decisive agent, since this is what produces modifications in the religious milieu, which in turn affect prayer. Nonetheless, it is true that the proximate causes are essentially religious. It is then generally within this well-defined subset of social phenomena that the comparison must be set in motion.

Such are the principal procedures to be used in the course of our study. In order to explain them they have to be separated from each other. But that does not mean that we shall use each one individually and consecutively. It would be a fruitless waste of argument if, each time a problem arose, we were to try to resolve it, not once and as a whole, but several times, according to the various divisions of our method. The one part of the argument that demands separate treatment is the provisional definition, because that is the first step on which all the rest depends. But after that, all the forms of criticism and all the comparative methods will naturally be combined in practice. The foregoing distinctions do not anticipate the framework of our exposition but are simply designed to clarify our position and to make it easier to verify our observations and hypotheses.

Chapter 3

Initial Definition

Thus the first task is to find a provisional definition of prayer. The aim is to discover an external but objective sign by which the phenomena of prayer may be recognized. For it must be clearly understood that our only object is to systematize such facts. When we say 'prayer' we are not implying that somewhere there exists a social entity which deserves this name and on which we could immediately speculate. An institution is not an indivisible unity, distinct from the facts that manifest it: it is merely their system. There is no such thing as 'religion', only particular religions. Moreover, each of these particular religions is merely a more or less organized set of beliefs and religious practices. Similarly, the word prayer is simply a noun by which is denoted a set of phenomena, each of which is itself a prayer. It is just that they all have in common certain particular characteristics which can be abstracted. Therefore we can group them under the same name which applies to all of them and not to anything else.

While we are seeking to establish this idea of prayer, we are in no way bound by current ideas; nevertheless, we should not do needless violence to those ideas. It is certainly not a question of giving a totally new meaning to a word in common use, but of replacing the usual, confused concept with a clearer and more distinct one. The physicist does not distort the meaning of the word heat when he defines it as expansion. Similarly, the sociologist will not distort the meaning of the word prayer by limiting its scope and sense. His only aim is to replace personal impressions with an objective sign which will dispel ambiguity and confusion and, while avoiding neologisms, will forestall mere playing with words.

But to define means to classify, that is, to situate an idea in relation to other ideas that have been previously defined. Now the science of religions has not yet applied itself sufficiently to produce a methodical classification of the facts with which it deals. Consequently, it hardly offers us any definitions to which we can refer. Hence we ourselves will have to define the phenomena by means of which we may express prayer. Of course in the present context, it can only be a question of provisional definitions, as it can be for prayer itself.

I. The rite

Prayer is usually classed among the rites of religion. This already gives us an initial element of the definition, provided at least that such a classification is acceptable. But in order to establish the soundness of this classification, we must first know what the word rite signifies. As the word is commonly used without being strictly defined, we shall have to make a definition ourselves.[93] Further, even if the current classification proves to be justified, it could not enlighten us about the characteristics of prayer unless the characteristics of a rite had already been defined.

Everyone will easily agree that rites are actions. The difficulty is to know what sort of actions they are.

Among the actions of religious life, there are some which are traditional, that is, they follow a form adopted by the group or by a recognized authority. Others, on the other hand – individual[94] ascetical practices for example – are strictly personal: they are not repeated and are not subject to any sort of regulation. The phenomena normally described as rites obviously belong to the first category. But even when they leave maximum room for individuality, there is always something regulated about them. Thus in the glossolalia* of the early Church, the neophyte in a state of trance gave free rein to his exclamations, to his jerky and mystic utterances as the Spirit moved him. It was an irregular mystical outpouring. But glossolalia found a place in the ritual of the mass, even becoming an integral part of it. It had to occur at a fixed time, which is why it is a rite.[95]

But not all traditional actions, however, are rites. Conventional acts of courtesy, along with those of a moral nature, have forms which are every bit as fixed as the most clearly defined rites. In fact they have often been confused with the latter. Moreover, this confusion is not without a certain foundation. It is in fact true that rites are linked with ordinary customs by an uninterrupted series of intermediate phenomena. Often something that is a custom in one place is a rite elsewhere: what was once a rite becomes a custom etc. Thus the

---

* Glossolalia or speaking with tongues is mentioned in the Acts of the Apostles 2, 2ff. Although it is much studied now one should not forget that psychologists and other scholars were also interested in the phenomenon in Mauss's day. See, for example, E. Lombard, *De la Glossolalie chez les premiers chrétiens et des phénomènes similaires. Etude d'exégèse et de psychologie*, 1910, Paris: Fischenbacher. See also note 95 by Mauss. [W.S.F.P.]

simple 'Good morning' which we find all over Europe, is a genuine, clearly formulated wish; nevertheless it has a merely conventional significance. On the other hand, the rules of courtesy as listed in Manu[96] as rites in the strict sense, vary according to the religious ranking of individuals. But what really differentiates them is that in the case of rules of courtesy, customs etc., the act is not efficacious in itself. This does not mean that its effects are nil. It simply means that its effects depend, principally or exclusively, not on its own qualities but on the fact that it is prescribed. For example, if I fail to greet someone, I offend them and risk being badly thought of; and if I greet them, I avoid any sort of trouble. But this playing for safety, this risk or giving of offence does not happen because the greeting is made up of particular gestures but simply because, under certain circumstances, I ought to greet them. On the other hand, for example, agrarian rites, are thought to have effects by virtue of the very nature of the practice. It is thanks to the rite that the plants grow. The power of the rite comes not only from the fact that it is performed in conformity with a given prescription; it comes also, and above all, from the rite itself. So a rite has a real material efficacy. In short, in this respect, the customs of a moral nature are in every way comparable to the practices followed in traditional games, songs and rounds, as well as adults' and children's dances, many of which, moreover, are survivals of ancient rites.[97] No doubt there is this difference between them, that in one case it is a serious act, in the other a game. But in both cases, if the act is given a particular form, it is not that this form has a special intrinsic value, it is simply that it is prescribed by rule. The Australians themselves make this distinction admirably. In certain tribes, when one local group meets another, they perform a *corroboree*, or more precisely, an *altertha*, a series of celebrations and dances which are even quite often totemic in character. But these types of celebration are in no way assimilated by the natives themselves in the grand ceremonies of the *intichiuma* (held by the totemic group), or to the rites of initiation, although there are very close resemblances between them. In the latter case the custom is observed in order to influence certain things, to increase the amount of food, the fertility of flowers etc. In the former, the practice is performed for its own sake. A rite is therefore an efficacious traditional action.

But there are traditional actions which are no less collective than rites, and which have perhaps a more marked efficacy, but which must nevertheless be distinguished from rites. These are industrial techniques. There is no need to demonstrate that they are efficacious and on the other hand, nothing could be more collective. They are determined by the tools in use in a given society, by the state of the economic division of labour etc. It is well known that societies can be characterised as much by their material civilization as by their language, legal system or religion. For example, the way in which fishermen divide up their work and combine their efforts, varies according to the development of technical skills, habitat, religious and magical beliefs, form of ownership, organization of the family etc. It is all the more important to distinguish all these things from rites because they are so closely linked with them in practice. So in hunting, fishing and agriculture, rites and techniques are intertwined to such an extent that we cannot distinguish the part played by each in the end result. A certain spring sacrifice contributes to the germination of the seeds just as much as the ploughing of the fields.[98] Sometimes it even happens that the rite is also a technique. In Polynesia, the taboo concerning the tops of coconut palms certainly arises from purely material and economic motives. Similarly, the Jewish *schechitah* is not only a means of killing animals but also a sacrifice.

We cannot distinguish these two kinds of things by observing the nature of the actions and their real effects. From that point of view, all we are able to say about rites is that they cannot produce the results attributed to them. In that case we would be unable to distinguish rites from erroneous practices. However, we know quite well that an erroneous practice is not a rite.[99] Hence, it is by considering not the efficacy in itself but the manner in which it is conceived, that we can discover the specific difference. Now in the case of a technique, the effect produced is believed to result entirely from effective mechanical work. And this is quite right because the endeavours of civilization have consisted in part in limiting to industrial techniques and sciences on which they are based, the useful powers formally attributed to rites and religious ideas. On the other hand, in the case of ritual practice, the expected result is attributed to the intervention of quite different causes. Between the acts that make up a foundation sacrifice for a house and the solidity that ostensibly results from it, there is no kind of mechanical relationship, even from the point of view of the person making the sacrifice.[100] The efficacy attributed to the rite has therefore nothing in common with the efficacy intrinsic to the actions which are physically performed. This efficacy is considered to be wholly *sui generis* because it is thought to proceed entirely from special powers which the rite has the ability to set in motion. Even when in fact the end product is the outcome of the actions performed, it is a rite if the believer attributes the result to other causes. Thus the consumption of toxic substances* produces a state of ecstasy by physiological means and yet it is a rite for those who impute this state not to its true causes but to special influences.[101]

But another distinction is necessary according to the nature of these forces. In certain cases they reside in the rite itself. It is the rite which creates and which *acts*. By its intrinsic quality, it has a direct influence over things. It is sufficient to itself. Thus purely through his incantations, his sympathetic, magical actions etc., the sorcerer makes rain and wind, stops a storm, gives life and death, casts or removes spells etc. It is as if the rite were possessed of immanent power, a sort of spiritual virtue. The rite has its own spirit, its mana

* i.e. hallucinogens.

as one says in Melanesia, because even the word spirit is too precise to translate this vague notion of creativeness. Rites which show only these characteristics can rightly be called magical.[102] But there are others which produce their results only through the intervention of certain forces which are believed to exist apart from the rite. These are sacred or religious forces, personal gods, general principles of vegetation, ill defined souls of totemic species etc. The rite is believed to work on these forces and through them to effect the course of events. It is not that the rite loses its special power but there are, in addition, other powers *sui generis* which contribute to the result and which are set in motion by the rite. Sometimes it is even these powers which contain the main creative principle and the rite merely calls it forth. We confine the word religious to rites of this kind. They can be distinguished from magic rites because they have one additional characteristic. They are efficacious with that efficacity intrinsic to the rite but they are so, both in themselves and through the mediation of the religious beings to whom they are addressed. Thus the Indian performs a magic rite when, on going hunting, he believes he is able to stop the sun by placing a stone at a certain height in a tree,[103] whereas Joshua performed a religious rite when, in order to stop the same sun, he invoked the omnipotence of Jahweh.

There are, moreover, as a corollary of the above, other external signs by which these two sorts of rite may be distinguished from each other. The first sort often exert their influence in a coercive way: they necessitate, they produce events with a certain determinism.[104] The second sort, by contrast, have often more of the contingent about them. They consist rather of solicitations by means of offerings or requests. The fact is, when one acts on a god, or even on an impersonal force like that of vegetation, the being through which the action is performed is not inert, as animals are, in the face of their destiny. It can always resist the rite, so one has to take it into account. Finally, what really makes us aware of the distance between the two types of practice is the fact that they are not accomplished by the same agents. It is the sorcerer or medicine man who as a rule performs magic. It is the religious group acting as a whole or through the intermediacy of its representatives, which is principally responsible for the cult of sacred things. And this distinction is to be found starting from the most primitive societies.

But in order to distinguish the two sorts of rite, we have considered them in their extreme forms. In reality they are species of the same genus between which there is a gap. In fact, between the entirely profane and the truly sacred, there is a whole series of intermediaries – demons, genies, fairies etc. These ambiguous beings are in some ways reminiscent of religious forces, but are of inferior quality. The sorcerer has a hold over them, he constrains them and subjugates them as he would profane things. Therefore, if the corresponding rites bear some resemblance to religious rites, they are nonetheless magical in character. There is not only a whole range of transitional forms between magic and religion, but the two can often only be distinguished by their place in the rituals and not by the way they work. There are some religious beings over whom people exercise as coercive a power as over demons or profane things. Conversely there are some demons with whom people employ procedures borrowed from the cult properly so-called. By a sympathetic ceremony, the Kangaroo clan constrains their totem, the kangaroo, to reproduce.[105] On the contrary there are genies to whom offerings and praises are given.[106] At other times we see a magic rite, which retains its magic nature, inserted into the course of a religious ceremony, or vice versa. In the course of the greatest Brahminic sacrifice, there appears a whole series of truly magical rites to bring about the death of an enemy, the welfare of cattle, to cure sterility in women etc.[107] Thus, it cannot be a question, as has been suggested,[108] of situating magic completely outside religious phenomena. Whilst acknowledging the links between them, however, we must not underestimate their very real differences. The rites of religion differ on account of the exclusively sacred character of the forces to which they are addressed. In conclusion, then, we can define them as *efficacious, traditional actions which have bearing on things that are called sacred.*

II. Prayer

We are now in a position to demonstrate that a considerable group of acts which everyone calls prayers, show all the characteristics of the religious rite as we have just defined it.

In the first place, every prayer is an act.[109] It is not just dreaming about a myth or simple speculation on dogma, but it always implies an effort, an expenditure of physical and moral energy in order to produce certain results. Even when it is entirely mental,[110] with no words spoken, with scarcely even a gesture, it is still a [voluntary] movement or an attitude of the soul.

Moreover, it is a traditional act inasmuch as it forms part of a ritual. We have seen besides that, even where it seems to be most free, it is still bound by tradition. In any case, if we came across religious acts which were like prayer in some respects but showed no trace of conformity, such an essential difference would oblige us to classify them separately and give them a different name.

Prayer is also efficacious and with a *sui generis* efficacy, for the words of prayer can give rise to the most extraordinary phenomena. Certain early rabbis by saying the appropriate *berakâ* (blessing), could change water into fire[111] and the great kings, by using certain formulae, could change impious Brahmins into insects which were then devoured by towns that had been changed into ant hills.[112] Even when all efficacy seems to have disappeared from prayer which has become pure adoration, or when all the power seems to be confined to a god, as in Catholic, Jewish or Islamic prayer, it is still efficacious because it causes the god to act in a certain way.

Finally, its efficacy is indeed that of religious rites because it is addressed to religious powers. By that very fact it is distinguishable from another similar activity with which it has often been confused – incantation. This also in fact consists of efficacious words. But, in principle, pure incantation is one simple thing: it makes no appeal to any force outside itself. It acts alone, it is the spell which is pronounced and then attaches itself directly to the bewitched object. Thus it is essentially a magical rite and we have a very easy way of distinguishing these two types of activity. We can say that prayer probably exists every time we encounter a text which specifically mentions a religious power. When it is not mentioned, we shall use the term 'prayer', if the place, circumstances and the agent of the rite have a religious character, that is, if it is performed in a sacred place, in the course of a religious ceremony or by a religious person. In other cases, we shall describe it as a purely magical incantation or as a mixed form.

But there are all sorts of degrees between incantations and prayers, as there are generally between the rites of magic and those of religion. Certain prayers in fact are real incantations in some aspects. For example, prayers which are used to consecrate necessarily effect the consecration. Conversely, certain incantations contain praises and petitions to the demons or gods to whom they are addressed. Again there are constant exchanges between the two domains. The help of high gods is sometimes sought in very minor magic rites. In India, Varuna intervenes in the magical cure of dropsy.[113] The most ancient mystical prayer in India may be found in the Atherva-Veda, the Veda of incantations. In the Rigveda[114] this prayer was used for a solar rite using sympathetic actions and can be interpreted either as a mystical exposition or as a series of riddles.[115] Sometimes it is the system of prayer which ends by annexing itself to the incantation. In this way the Berakhoth tracts in the Mishna and the Talmuds[116] are as a rule made up of real incantations, which have nothing religious about them except at the beginning the invocation of Yahweh. The Atherva-Veda, excluded for a long time from the domain of the Vedas, ended by being assimilated into it. That is, it too became a collection of religious formulae, one of the pillars on which the world was believed to rest.[117] In fact, what is prayer for one church often becomes a magical formula for the adherents of another church.

Since, then, these two sorts of rite are so closely related, since there is constant intercommunication so that they are, as it were, in a state of continual osmosis, it is obvious that it will be impossible to separate them radically in the course of our study. We must even expect to find plenty of ambiguous elements which it will be impossible to classify with any precision. If we were to confine ourselves to a consideration of prayer *stricto sensu*, we would run the risk of finding here and there prayers for which we could not identify an origin and others which disappeared without our knowing where they had gone. Moreover, as religious and magical elements in any given society are part of the same system and perhaps have the same source, a comparative study is bound to be of interest. However, it was nonetheless necessary to distinguish them by an objective sign; for that is the only possible way to indicate the place of prayer and incantation respectively, while determining the links between them.

But religious rites as a whole should be divided into two large groups: some are manual, the rest are oral. The first consist in movements of the body and of objects, the second in ritual locutions. It is obvious that speech has a totally different power of expression from gestures, and that since it is made up not of movements but simply of words, it cannot owe its efficacy to the same causes. Prayer is obviously an oral rite. This does not mean that there are not some doubtful cases which are occasionally difficult to classify. Thus one could reasonably hold that there is nothing verbal in mental prayer. In reality, however, an interior prayer is still a prayer and for there to be language it is not necessary that the words be physically pronounced. It is still an action of the mind.[118] Then again, there are certain manual rites, clearly symbolic, that could be called prayers because they are in fact a sort of sign language. For example, all religious dramas whose purpose is to represent the great deeds of the gods, their battles against the demons etc., constitute behaviour equivalent to the prayer chants which recount to the gods their own story and incite them to repeat their exploits. They are only on the periphery of prayer, however, as sign language is on the periphery of articulated language: consequently we shall not include them in our definition. On the other hand, there are certain oral rites which we shall consider as prayers although they have become mechanical through a series of degradations. This is what we have called the regressions of prayer. In fact they are always oral in origin and it is the words which give them their potency.

But all oral religious rites are not prayers: take for example, the oath, the verbal contract in a religious wedding, the religiously-founded wish, the blessing or curse, the vow, the oral dedication etc. One essential characteristic distinguishes them. Their principal effect consists in modifying the state of a profane thing which is to be endued with a religious character. An oath or a ritual contract[119] is intended above all to consecrate an utterance that has been made, placing it beneath the sanction of the witnessing gods. By the religiously-founded wish, an event acquires the power that will assure its realization.[120] In the case of a blessing or curse, it is a person who is blessed or cursed. In the vow or dedication[121] the promise or the presentation causes something to pass into the sphere of the sacred. Without doubt all these rites set in motion religious powers which help to give this new quality to what is declared, wished or vowed. The end result of the act is not the influence acquired over religious things but the change of condition effected in the profane thing.

Prayer, on the contrary, is above all a means of acting upon sacred beings; it is they who are influenced by prayer, they who are changed. It is not that prayer has no repercussions in the everyday domain. Further, there is probably no rite that does not benefit the worshipper in some way. When one prays, one usually expects some result from one's prayer, for something or someone, even if it is only for oneself.[122] But this is only a by-product and does not dominate the actual mechanism of the rite. This last is directed entirely to the religious powers to whom the rite is addressed and it is only secondarily, by their mediation, that the rite comes to affect ordinary life. Sometimes even its only real use is the simple comfort it brings to the one who prays: nearly all its efficacy is absorbed by the divine realm.

However, the difference between prayer and other oral religious rites is not so clear-cut that one can say precisely where one starts and the others end. A prayer can serve as an oath;[123] a wish can take the form of a prayer. A supplication can be interwoven within a benediction. One can vow something to a god with a formula that is clearly petitionary. But if the boundaries between these two areas of religious life tend to be uncertain, they are nonetheless distinct, and it was important to make this separation in order to avoid possible confusion.

So we come finally to the following definition: *prayer is a religious rite which is oral and bears directly on the sacred.*[124*]

---

* French, *les choses sacrées*.

BOOK II

THE NATURE OF ELEMENTARY ORAL RITES

Chapter 1

History of the Question and Delineation of the Subject

Now that we have established a definition of the oral religious rite, and in particular of prayer, we can enter into a discussion of the one problem which was posed in this first study: that of the origins of prayer. It will also oblige us to address the more general problem of the origin of belief in religious formulae in societies of a primitive structure.

I

If, as has been observed, there is a paucity of scientific literature about prayer in general, that concerning the special question we have in mind is even more meagre. It is difficult to cite even a few names.

Of the two philosophers of religion whose views we have discussed, Sabatier after a rapid survey skirts the problem without even seeking to establish the truth of the facts. He does not ascertain whether prayer as he understands it, that is, conceived as 'religion in act and spirit', is in fact the universal phenomenon which he says it is.[125] The other, Tiele,[126] confines himself to making dialectical objections to those who seek to deduce primitive prayer from theurgic formulae. In support of his theory he cites only a number of very refined formulae from already highly developed religions.[127] Besides, both of them,[128] like most philosophers of religion, are hardly concerned with seeking the form and exact meaning of rites in primitive societies. All their work tends towards criticism or to showing the excellence of certain religious states of mind.

Among the anthropologists, only Tylor, Farrer and Max Müller[129] have considered the question.

Tylor held that prayer started by being a simple and immediate expression of a material desire and would have been addressed to supernatural powers, to spirits whose origin was explained by animism. The North American Indians would be at precisely this stage of development of the institution, while the ancient Hindus, the Greeks and the Romans had not entirely passed beyond it. But Tylor, writing at a time when anthropology and sociology were just being founded, lumped all these primitive peoples together in one huge genus, without species or hierarchies. Thus he began with rituals which were obviously very advanced[130] in societies which were already highly civilized. Besides, on account of his animistic theory, he imagined that people started out with the concept of personalities that were at once spiritual and divine – a concept which, in our opinion, is a late idea, fostered precisely by the earliest forms of prayer.

Max Müller's theory[131] is in part identical with that of Tylor, in part with that of Farrer. The philologist has, in this instance, assumed the role of anthropologist. He starts with facts about the Melanesians which were recently noted by Codrington,[132] and his comments are not without importance. He espies clearly that, apart from what we usually term prayers, there are different forms equally deserving of the name. In the course of a rapid review of the different forms that prayer can take, he suggests that prayer began with expressions such as 'may *my* will be done' and ended with the exact opposite: 'may *your* will be done'.[133] According to him, Semitic and Vedic prayers were staggered between these two contrasted poles. But such brilliant expositions cannot take the place of proof. Firstly, although the formulae quoted are indeed primitive in character, they co-exist, according to Codrington, with other prayers of a precise supplicatory nature,[134] and also there is in fact nothing to prove that some are more primitive than others, and that injunction preceded invocation. Secondly, the basic problem concerning prayer remains to be addressed. How can words possess power, how can they give orders to a divine being? That is what remains incomprehensible, especially if one accepts Max Müller's views on the origin of religion as a universal sense of the infinite, common to all mankind. In fact it is difficult to understand how Max Müller failed to notice the serious contradiction between his two doctrines: for if prayer began with incantation or magic, it means that the divinity was by no means conceived as the representation of infinite grandeur and morality.

In short, Max Müller[135] adhered to an interesting thesis of one of the pioneers in this field, Farrer,[136] who is somewhat forgotten these days. Having studied the customs of North American Indians, Africans and Polynesians, Farrer maintained that the prayer of 'savages' was originally magic incantation. But on the one hand, the rituals on which he bases his discussion contain something very different from magic incantation. They contain important oral rites that can certainly not be classed under that heading. And, on the other hand, the very advanced societies with highly developed religions which he studied could not provide him either with sufficiently primitive data, or with the means of addressing the fundamental question of the efficacy of words.

It appears however that, apart from Tylor, there is a certain unanimity on the question of the primitive incantatory form of prayer. Two recent works by Marett[137] and Rivers[138] in fact consider this theory as an established truth: Marett sees all religious evolution extending from incantation to prayer, which he confines to petition. Rivers makes some interesting comments on the liturgy of the Todas[139] which he considers as purely magical. He regards the Todas as a primitive people but is well aware, however, that they are able to distinguish formulae that are truly malificent.

Starting from Marett's work and documents, a historian of Greek religion, Farnell, has recently written a book on the development of religion in which he advances several hypotheses on the 'history of prayer'.[140] He differs from his predecessors, however, on one point. If he admits, like them, that there can be peoples without prayers, whose oral rites are limited to incantations, he nevertheless believes that, from the very start, an opposition existed between incantation and pure prayer, in which the god was invoked as a relative or friend. He thinks that one should classify religions according to the proportion of incantations and prayers which, he maintains, they all contain. Later on we shall have to question this theory quite often, so at this point we need not embark on a debate which would presuppose a full examination of the facts. Let it suffice that we have indicated its link with the hypothesis currently in favour.

However, all these theories are guilty of grave defects of method. In the first place, if oral rites started as magic, how and why did prayer emerge from them? Why do nature and the gods cease to be dependent on the voice of man?[141] Because experience reveals the failures of the rite? But apart from the fact that belief in magic itself is founded precisely on the impossibility of being put to the test like that,[142] no explanation is given as to why, having ceased to constrain these powers, people start to invoke them instead of simply ceasing to address them at all. Secondly, all these studies fail to throw light on the origin not only of prayer but also of incantation, the possibility of which needs to be explained. To maintain that an oral spell or a request addressed to a spirit is the primitive form of prayer, is not a sufficient explanation of how that spell could have been thought effective, of how that request could have been thought to lead to results or to serve some useful purpose. Thirdly, all these authors start from premature comparisons. None of them describes for us a liturgical system consisting entirely of incantation. None of them makes a study of sufficiently primitive data. Without such study we cannot be sure that there are not other forms, closer to what we can imagine as the primary forms of the institution. It is this threefold fault that we must avoid.

II

To this end, we must choose as a terrain for our research a group of well defined societies where oral ritual is present under the following conditions: 1) it should have a religious character sufficiently pronounced for us to be sure if or when the ritual is not composed solely of pure prayers but of more complex rites, that we may derive prayer from these rites with no unbridgeable gaps in our deductions; 2) the oral ritual must be observable under the sort of conditions which make it possible to offer an explanation of the rite, that is, to develop with some chance of success, a hypothesis on the origin of the faith placed in them; 3) one must be quite sure that, in these societies, there are no other forms of oral rite apart from these primitive forms, and that it is not possible to find, so far as present knowledge goes, phenomena of a more elementary nature.

We believe that the observation of Australian societies[143] meets these three requirements. The rest of this study will be devoted to proving the point. But it is useful at this stage to show briefly that we could not find a more favourable terrain for our research.

In the first place, among currently observable societies or those known historically, we know of none that presents to the same degree incontestable signs of a primitive and elementary organization. Small, poor, sparse, technologically backward, stagnant from a moral and intellectual viewpoint, with the most archaic social structures imaginable, they even help us to form a schematic view of the first human societies from which all others developed – notwithstanding the long history we must imagine lying behind them.* We cannot go so far as Schœtensack[144] who, in a sort of anthropological drunkenness, maintains that they are the original primitives; who, having remained in the cradle of the human race, at the very place where human beings evolved, have never needed to innovate or evolve further. Nevertheless, we know of only two groups of so-called primitives who give us the impression that their history started at such a low level and has been so little influenced by the rise and fall of races, civilizations and societies. First we have the Aghans of Tierra del Fuego[145] but they have more or less disappeared now, before having been systematically described;[146] and perhaps they were degenerate rather than truly primitive. Then there are the Seri Indians of the Island of Tiburon in the Gulf of California. But we find MacGee's monograph superficial;[147] the author spent little time among them and they remain overall almost unknown; besides, if they appear to be primitive in some respects,[148] they also seem to have a long history behind them,[149] and their language and race clearly links them with the large

---

* This is an important sentence for understanding Mauss's brand of evolutionism. See N.J. Allen, *Categories and Classifications: Maussian Reflections on the Social*, 2000, New York and Oxford: Berghahn, p. 20.

American group of the Yumas, Pimas, Papagos etc.[150] The other sections of humankind usually considered primitive are not so in fact. Even the African pygmies[151] and the Negritoes of Malaysia[152] who are obviously extremely 'savage',* live in the midst of great barbarian civilizations – Bantu and Nilotic in Africa, Malayo-Polynesian in Malaya; and they participate to a certain extent in those civilizations. As for the Veddas[153] and the Asiatic savages, the theories constructed on the meagreness of their civilization and lack of religion have been refuted.

Not only do the Australian societies show signs of primitiveness, but they are still both numerous and homogeneous enough, while also sufficiently different from each other, to form a group which is eminently suitable for research into a complete body of ritual and its variations. Although their habitation extends across a whole continent, they do in fact form a sort of whole, a sort of ethnic unity, incorrectly termed a 'geographic province' as Bastian used to say.[154] This is to say that they have a single civilization, they form a family of societies linked not only by history, identity, technology, language, art, legal and religious systems,[155] but also by race,[156] so that a certain number of propositions applicable to some of them will be likely to apply to others. If there are variations, they operate on a common underlying basis, in which they all come together. Thus comparisons within the group can be made with a minimum of risk. And so, while acknowledging the local colour of the data – their Australianness – at least during our descriptive study, we shall be able to satisfy both the demands of science, which compares, and of historical ethnography, which seeks to be specific.

But this homogeneity does not exclude a certain heterogeneity. Within Australian civilization, distinctions† have been made between several currents or several types.[157] On the other hand, scholars have distinguished, almost with unanimity and above all correctly, religious phenomena in various stages of *evolution*.[158] The debate centres on which rank to assign to the various societies. We ourselves will be obliged to address the question. But it is of little importance at this point. For the purposes of our study it suffices that there should be no doubt about the diversity itself. It is enough if we have to convey the firm impression that the societies we are going to study are neither all at the same level, nor uniform, nor all oriented in the same directions. For if underlying these variations we can constitute a type of primitive oral rite, and if we can establish its probable universality among this mass of diverse societies, then we shall have hit upon a necessary phenomenon for societies of this type. At the same time, the variations in scale, form, content, even religious style, to which this type of rite will be subject, will often be no less interesting to

* Mauss is referring implicitly to the then recognized classification – savages, barbarians, civilized.

† French text reads *dédaigné*. This is surely a misprint for *distingué*.

observe than the general type itself. Being dependent themselves on definite social phenomena, these variations will be susceptible to explanation, and such explanations will then contribute to the general explanation.

We should add that Australian societies are beginning to be among the best known of those which are generally called primitive. Not only have the latest expeditions of Spencer and Gillen[159] and the latest researches of Roth[160] been conducted with all the resources of modern ethnography. And not only is the research currently being published by missionaries from the central area directed by one of the finest ethnographical museums,[161] but there is also great value in the oldest documents, those of Howitt, first published, little by little, and then brought out together, and to some extent filled out in a single volume.[162] And certain parts of the old books by Woods,[163] Grey[164] and Eyre[165] are just as valuable as the best contemporary works. What is more, we are beginning, as much with the help of the old linguists as with the more recent ones,[166] to form a fairly accurate idea of the structure of the Australian languages, their thought forms and powers of expression. Finally, we possess a sufficient number of texts of myths and formulae in juxtalinear translation (see chaps III, IV and V below) to ensure that this study of primitive prayer will continue to be of value when the philology of Australian languages has been finally established.

It is not that all the facts are known, nor are all the known facts well known. We still need to be prepared for some surprises, such as that occasioned by the appearance of the first book by Spencer and Gillen. Some scholars have yet to recover from it, and remain, so to speak, fascinated by the Arunta. Other comparable discoveries could overturn a certain number of our ideas and we can indeed expect some, since out of the two hundred and fifty Australian societies which Curr counted, including those now extinct, but excluding many as yet unknown tribes, only about thirty are known with varying degrees of accuracy. However, as the firsthand documents which we have been able for the most part to examine, bear on societies spread across the whole continent, with the most diverse social and religious structures, we believe that any possible discoveries will not provide any data entirely contradictory to those we are going to study. Then again, despite the diverse and varying authority of the evidence we shall bring forward, they come from such varied sources and can be checked one against another so readily that their critical assessment seems easy.

But before going on to the description and then the explanation of primitive forms of prayer in Australia and so, by hypothesis, of prayer in general,* we need to answer a fundamental objection to which we personally attach no importance but which might be speciously brought against us. What right have

---

* Mauss is contrasting data-based examination of Australia with hypothetical extrapolation. He 'in general' foreshadows the last two words of the paragraph.

we thus to choose in this way between the various facets of prayer? What right do we have to deduce, from prayer in Australian religions, the origins of prayer in general?

It is certain that the only methodical way to establish that Australian prayer is a sample of the original type of prayer would be to show that all other forms of prayer evolved from formulae similar to the Australian type. Obviously such a demonstration cannot be attempted in the course of a single work. However, in the absence of such proof, which alone could be decisive, there are very good reasons that allow us for the time being to regard the facts we are going to study as primitive. Firstly, we are observing these facts in the least developed societies known to us. So there is every chance that the religious phenomena we there encounter will have the same primitive character as the other social phenomena. Secondly, we shall see that Australian prayer is closely linked to the totemic system, that is, to the most archaic religious system hitherto discovered by history and ethnography. Lastly and most important, we shall show that, while it is quite different from what we usually call by that name, Australian prayer nevertheless contains all the essential elements of the more complex and refined rites to which idealist religions give the name prayer. At the same time, by its simplicity, even its crudeness, Australian oral ritual obviously takes us back to the first phases of religious development. It is even difficult to imagine how any simpler ritual could exist. In it we discover the whole future in germaine form. So it is at least a strong presumption that this future development did in fact spring from such a source.

Moreover, it is clear that any conclusions to which we may be led can only be provisional. Scientific conclusions are always of this kind and the scholar must always be ready to revise them. If anyone discovers a more elementary form of prayer or establishes that, under specific conditions, prayer first came into being in a more complex form, that will be the moment to examine the facts that can be advanced in support of one or other assertion. For the moment it is enough to say that no simpler form has yet been reached by analysis and, conversely, that all the more developed forms of prayer known to us are manifestly the product of a more or less lengthy historical evolution.

Chapter 2

Do Prayers Exist in Australia?

I

When we pose the question in this form, we encounter two contradictory positions. According to some, not only does prayer exist in Australia but it already has the form of supplication or invocation, an appeal addressed to a powerful and independent divinity, just as is found in the most advanced religions.[167] According to others, on the contrary, the Australians know of nothing that might be called by the name of prayer.[168] Let us examine in turn the documents on which each of these assertions is based.

Among the reports relied upon by those who believe they have found prayers, in the European sense of the word, in Australia, some are so obviously totally worthless that they need not detain us.[169] Other, more credible reports are completely lacking in supporting evidence.[170] They are confined to simple assertions, without a single text from a formula to support them. Others, which seem more precise and apparently contain the beginnings of a real demonstration, are basically the result of simple confusions or misuse of nomenclature. With reference to tribes which are this time well localized, certain authors use the words 'invocation', 'adjuration', 'supplication' where they could prove only the existence of an oral rite, probably a very simple one. When Oxley[171] tells us that the Sydney tribe[172] prayed, he says nothing precise; when Heagney speaks of adjuration addressed to invisible spirits, in order to cast a spell on someone, or of supplication to produce rain, he is guilty of a veritable misuse of language. When Peechey[173] talks of propitiation and invocation with regard to what he himself calls 'corroborees', that is, sung dances 'for rain', he is abusing his role of interpreter. None of these words is used with adequate justification.

Of greater importance are the documents published by Mrs Langloh Parker on the Euahlayi.[174] She speaks of a funeral ceremony containing a sort of prayer to Baiame, the great creator god of all the tribes of the grasslands.[175] In this prayer the spirit of the departed was commended to the god who was begged to allow the dead, who had been faithful to his laws, faithful on earth, to enter the heavenly abode called *Bullimah*, the 'land of beauty';[176] and to save him from *Eleanbah wundah*,[177] or hell. The prayer is pronounced by the senior medicine-man or *wirreenun*, who stands facing east, bowing his head like all those present.[178]

However illustrious Mrs Parker's affirmation may be, it seems to us highly contestable. Firstly, the very nature of the formulae used betrays a Christian origin, a borrowing, at least indirectly, from Biblical, indeed Protestant, language. 'O Baiame, hear our cry'.[179] Secondly, there are all sorts of reasons to suspect that the tribe under observation was at least in a state of receptivity which would incline it to imitations of this kind. It had been in the process of dissolution since Mrs Parker's youth;[180] it contained many foreign elements[181], and they at least could certainly have been exposed to a degree of evangelization. Further, as our observer grew up more or less living among them and only later thought of noting down and publishing her observations, which are undated, everything leads us to believe that this description is of a recent practice, subsequent to the direct or indirect influence of white people. One cannot but be reminded of the European custom at the time of a burial, which requires the deceased's relatives to stand in a circle with heads bowed. Besides,[182] this isolated report will seem even more unlikely when one realizes that the prayer *for* the dead (and not *to* the dead) is certainly one of the rarest, most refined, and most recent of all forms of oral rite. It is only in Christianity that we can be sure of its presence and even then only in a far from primitive form of Christianity.[183] It is therefore unlikely that the Australians, without any outside help, should have covered, in one bound, all the intermediate stages which separated them from these complex and elevated forms of prayer. Also, there is absolutely nothing to prove that this custom was observed constantly either before or after Mrs Parker's observations. We believe we have proof that the Euahlayi did in fact change their funeral rites during the course of Mrs Parker's presence among them. In fact, describing the burial of the venerable Eerin, the author does not mention an important rite which she tells us about in her account of the burial of old Beemunny – a woman to whom however less respect to her was paid than to the mortal remains of a man. We refer to a rite, which is certainly very Australian, the funeral chant sung over the grave in which all the names of the deceased are called to mind, together with his totems and sub-totems.[184] The alternative is, we accept, as Mrs Parker seems to do, that the ritual is very different for men and women[185] and that for the women Baiame was not invoked and for the men totems were not invoked. This seems to us unlikely. For, at the very least, the two rites should have been used at men's funerals if there had not been important changes in the cult of the dead at a considerably earlier period.

Mrs Parker vouches for another, equally circumstantial instance of prayer to Baiame, although admittedly she did not witness it directly because it was a case of initiation and she never attended a *boorah*.[186] This is what it consists of. At his second initiation,[187] the young man is allowed to see the representations of the great god Baiame and his wife Birragnooloo:[188] these figures are carved on trees, moulded in relief on the ground and traced on the grass. He hears the sacred chant of Baiame[189] and then she tells us the youth finally hears the prayer addressed to Baiame by the senior medicine-man or *wirreenuns* who is present.[190] He 'asks' Baiame 'to allow the black men to live on earth for a long time because they have faithfully observed his laws, as can be seen from their observance of the boorah.' 'The senior medicine-man repeats these words several times in the posture and tone of a supplicant, facing the east, the direction in which the dead are buried.' But one wonders if the author's interpretation of these words spoken by a native is not a little forced, or if there is not a certain willingness to oblige that has been blended into the wording of the native informant. The language of the formula is very biblical.[191] We may be dealing simply with a rite which was very common in that region of Australia but which does not constitute a prayer of the type indicated by Mrs Parker. In all these tribes of central and south New South Wales, the old men engage in a sort of demonstration of the existence of the great god Baiame or of some other celestial god,[192] which is not only artistic, using painting, sculpture, drawings, but is also spoken. There are even a number of these initiation ceremonies where one or several old men often buried and as if on the point of being re-born,[193] enter into conversation with the great god. The old man asks and answers questions, sometimes from the tomb, as if he were a spirit conversing with another spiritual being. In all these cases, we do indeed have prayers in the general sense that we have defined prayer, but we are far from that formula – somewhere between a creed, a Lord's Prayer and an echo of the Decalogue – which Mrs Parker places on the lips of the senior medicine-man. Besides, if the rite ever existed, it must have been of recent date, because it had not yet found a place in the myth of the first bora, instituted by Baiame himself and described elsewhere;[194] this myth, on which all the liturgy is based, makes no mention of Baiame commanding men to pray to him when they obeyed his laws.

In fact, we find all Mrs Parker's observations slightly suspect. They may have been tainted by a preconceived idea. For our author states as a principle that there can be no people or religion without prayer.[195] One can see the danger of such a principle of research, which led Mrs Parker to emphasize certain features of a ritual of dubious antiquity.

The opposite theory is held by some of the best ethnographical authorities. One of these is Curr[196] who had an intimate knowledge of quite a number of tribes, from Queensland to the Lower Murray. Howitt is in no less radical disagreement.[197] As for Spencer and Gillen, they go even further than Curr in maintaining that in all the tribes of central Australia, they have never even found the ideas necessary for the formation of prayer;[198] they vouch for the magical character of all the oral and manual rites of the Arunta and of the other tribes in their domain.[199]

Beside these observers, familiar with many Australian societies, there is a group of others who are no less definite in their views and no less precise. Stephens on the Adelaide tribe,[200] Semon on those of south Queensland,[201] Mrs Smyth describing the Boandik of south-west Victoria,[202] Mann, drawing on the experience of a resident (T. Petrie[203]), who had spent a long time with the Moreton Bay tribe.[204] Finally, with regard to the southern tribes of western Australia, we have the valuable denials of a Catholic bishop, founder of the mission of New Norcia. He believes that Motagon is the benign creator god and that this idea corresponds with primitive revelation,[205] but he admits that the god was in no way revered, either by prayer or offerings.

An even more serious indication than these explicit denials, the result of research that is likely to have been conscientious, is the fact that in the Australian languages for which we possess the vocabularies, lexicons or texts, for example, translations of the Bible, we find nothing which suggests the word prayer.[206] Even where this word was needed, for example, for evangelism, it was necessary to introduce foreign words, or hammer out new words or change the meaning of other words. And this is not only to make Christian rites comprehensible, but also to translate the Old Testament itself. In the Gospels and Genesis in Awabakal, translated by the admirable Threlkeld, the words which replace 'pray' and 'prayer' are composed with the aid of a verb root *wya* which means simply to speak.[207] In Gason's Dieri vocabulary, the sole word which comes close to prayer means only incantation.[208] The little lexicon produced by Thomas, the protector of the natives of Victoria,[209] shows the Europeans simply grafting the word thank onto the languages of the Bunurong, Wurnjerri etc. in order to express 'thanksgiving' to the divinity and creating (we do not know how) a new word 'pardogurrabun' to signify a vow.

But these definite denials and this disquieting silence on the part of the language itself are not enough to prove the absence of any kind of prayer. We must in fact take into account the prejudices of European ethnographers, missionaries and even philologists. The distinctions made here can be understood in the light of arbitrary confusions elsewhere. Even the biblical texts where for the Hebrew, prayer was no more than a solemn word, a means of access to the divinity who was unapproachable except through the established forms, sound to the ears of a Protestant or Catholic missionary like edifying outpourings of the soul. Neither these negations nor this silence are enough to prove the absence of any kind of prayer.

The fact that these different observers found not the least trace of prayer may be due to other causes. It is obvious that they start from the same assumption as those who hold the opposite view. For them, Christian prayer, or at least prayer conceived as a spiritual interchange between the believer and his god, is the basic model of prayer. Under the influence of this prejudice, they were unable to recognize the common ground between such a concept of prayer and the sort of words which the Australian addresses to his sacred domestic spirits. It is, moreover, for the same reason that Spencer and Gillen refuse to see, in the system of rites and totemic beliefs, a religion properly so-called. So their negative conclusion, in the case in point, lacks the authority usually associated with their testimony. In order to discover prayer in Australia, we need to reduce it to its essential elements and to learn how to avoid seeing all religious matters through Christian eyes.

The alleged poverty of the vocabulary is no more conclusive an argument. These field-workers were attempting to make the language express the idea of prayer according to their preconceived notions; naturally it refused to do so, as this idea was foreign to the natives. The word for prayer was lacking, as was the actual thing. To men imbued with theological ideas, whether elementary or advanced, as were the authors of these linguistic studies, it was impossible to bridge the gap separating their idea of the language suitable for addressing God and the sort of words used by the Australian aborigines when addressing their totems and spirits. The observers were naturally incapable of perceiving the common ground between a Christian prayer and an incantation intended to charm an animal. This accounts for their disclaimers. And if the language is incapable of expressing the missionary's idea of prayer, it is quite simply that these languages and religions were not ready for the form of prayer which he wanted to teach; but this does not mean that other systems of prayer were not in use.

What are these other systems? That is what we are now going to show.

II. The beginnings

What we find are not in any degree – and to this extent we have to agree with the negative theory – prayers of adoration, self-abasement, mental outpourings. But there do exist prayers of another kind or of other kinds. In the interwoven system of Australian cults, there are numerous oral rites which deserve the name if one adopts the sufficiently general definition which we suggested above. Having accepted that, one can see how rudimentary oral rites can have the nature and functions of prayer without attaining the moral status, the psychological value or the semantic content of the religious discourse which we usually attach to this name.

But there is more. Even in Australian religions one can perceive, not only the mass of forms that are elementary, confused and complex, but also faint outlines and beginnings, attempts at a more finished mode of expression. The institution, which has already come to life, starts haltingly to stammer in the rhythms which will later come to articulate the whole oral rite. Naturally all these customs differ only in nuances from the general type of oral rites which we shall establish later on. But as in the egg there appears the spot of blood – the nucleus from which the chick will develop – so here and there in Australia there emerge, in various degrees of colouring, attempts at prayer in the European sense of the word. These attempts will enable us to understand the process leading to the birth of that particular species to which observers and scholars have believed they could reduce the whole genus. They will help us look in the right place to discover the laws of an evolution. Finally, they will convey the feeling that, even if there is a considerable distance between Australian oral practices and even those of ancient religions, there have existed and continue to exist logical connections between the two sorts of ritual. For phenomena, such as those we are going to describe, would have been impossible if the remainder of the oral ritual of our primitive Australians had not possessed any trace of the generic characteristics of prayer and had been mere incantation.

Later on, we shall attribute more importance, and indeed their full value, to rain-making rites. But now we can detach from this fuller study certain documents that merit attention now. It is indeed easy to understand why even to observers, who were intimately acquainted with the natives, rites of this type should have given the impression of being true European prayers. Whether they seek to drive away rain or cause it to fall, the rites obviously express the desire, the need and the moral and material distress of a whole group of people. The words are easily understood as a sort of prayer or wish. And since rain and water are usually conceived as residing somewhere, say in a place where they can be made to come forth, the formulae appear to be addressed to a personal power whose coming or mysterious aid is invoked. It is important to fix the limit behind which these rites can be classified – a limit beyond which in Australia they have not passed.[210]

Bunce[211] tells us that[212] during a storm, when they arrived at the camp, 'a group of old men started to pray for good weather; their prayer consisted of a continuous, melancholy chant. They continued this ritual activity for some time', but finding that their god was, for the moment, deaf to their appeals, they cried: 'Marmingatha bullarto porkwadding; quanthunura – Marmingatha is very sullen: why?'.[213] In spite of the precise terms used, we see here only a prayer of quite another kind from that envisaged by Bunce. It is clear that in this case there was an oral rite; words and phrases were chanted. But we do not have the formula used and there is nothing to prove that it had a precatory character. In fact, what followed the rite would rather imply the opposite interpretation. For, seeing their lack of success, the old men 'spat into the air in the direction of the storm, shouting at it with scorn'.[214] So it is very likely that the first words addressed to Marmingatha were orders rather than marks of respect, since the same spiritual personage is exposed to insults. Besides, even if there had indeed been a prayer at that moment, and not simply a rite which was so interpreted, we could deduce nothing from it. The Geelong tribe, established at that time in its reservation, had already been evangelized. This can be seen by the very use of the word *marmingatha* according to Bunce's own vocabulary.[215] The word, which probably meant a father,[216] an ancestor, at the very most a spirit,[217] thus designates everything pertaining to evangelical religion – the people (*personnel*), God, actions and especially prayer.

Other oral rites of the same class are subject to the same analytic reduction. For example, the children's prayers for rain in the Euahlayi tribe are at the most a sort of magic circle.[218] Similarly, when Gason thought that the Dieri tribe called upon Moora Moora, the creator god, and prayed to him for rain,[219] he simply misunderstood both the nature of the deity invoked and the nature of the formula, which we now possess.[220] All that was involved were the totemic ancestors of a rain clan; the prayers addressed to them have very little to do with the system of Christian invocation.[221]

So we must look elsewhere for clearer and more precise evidence.[222] In a certain number of tribes, completely isolated from each other, the name of the totems[223] is articulated in the same way as is the divine person in much more highly developed religions. The auxiliary animal is present to its worshipper in reality and in spirit. 'In the Mallanpara tribe,[224] on retiring and going to sleep or on rising, one must pronounce, in a more or less low voice, the name of the animal etc. of which one is the namesake, or that is associated with the group to which one belongs,[225] adding the words "wintcha, wintcha" – where? where? (are you?)'. If appropriate, (that is, if this is the usage that exists in other contexts),[226] one should imitate the noise or cry or call (of the animal).[227] The aim of this practice, taught by the elders to the young as soon as they are old enough to learn these things, is to make them lucky and skilful in hunting and to help them receive useful warnings of every danger[228] that the animal (etc.) might give them. If a man with the name of a fish invokes it regularly in this way, he will be a successful fisherman and, should he be hungry, he will catch a large fish.[229] If an individual neglects to call on thunder, rain, etc.,[230] assuming of course, that they are his namesakes, he will lose power to make them act.[231] Snakes, alligators etc. will not trouble their namesakes, when they are regularly evoked (*sic*) without giving some warning, a sign, a 'something' that the aborigine feels inside his stomach or a tingling sensation in his legs. If the individual neglects this practice, it will be his own fault if he is caught or bitten.[232] 'This calling-up of name-sakes is not supposed to benefit the women very much. If people were to call upon others than their name-sakes, under the circumstances above mentioned, it would bear no results either for good or harm'.[233]

In another Queensland tribe there is a similar practice which we would have been inclined to classify with this appeal to the totem. 'These people, before going to sleep, call out one or other of the names of the animals, plants and things linked to the primary division of the tribe to which they belong.[234] The animal or thing thus called upon, warns the sleepers at night of the approach of other animals etc.' In other words, if we have rightly understood these obscure sentences, the auxiliary animal[235] watches over the one who is protected and warns him of everything that could happen to him through the agency of beings that are subsumed or classified into other matrimonial classes. For example, let us suppose that a Kurchilla oppossum receives information from the oppossum, which is of the same class, that it is just about to rain. Rain is sacred to the Wungko. But we are not sure that it is really a matter of totems here, because there is no reference to clans bearing these names nor to any cult addressed, outside these rites – to these species* and things, including the wind and the rain. However it is very likely to be so. In the whole group of neighbouring tribes there exists precisely a very special type of totemism in which the people of the totem and those linked to its class are the only ones permitted to eat the totem and the totems of their class[236] and in which the food prohibitions in consequence go according to the classes,[237] food and worship being so to speak divided with a minimum of co-operation between the two phratries. We should make allowance for the fact that Roth has what we consider a systematic tendency, which he admits, not to see totems anywhere, even where there certainly exist[238] families named after animals or things and exercising a singular power over them.

This phenomenon, though rare, is not however isolated. We find the practice in the Parnkalla tribe of Port Lincoln (Southern Australia)[239] in a form of the rite that is intermediate between the two rites that we have just described. Here, the names of the totems are shouted out during the hunt; if it is successful, the men strike their stomachs saying 'Ngaitye paru! Ngaitye paru!', 'my meat, my meat' in Schürmann's translation.[240] Other formulae, on the contrary, do not seem to be restricted to members of the totemic clan but to those of other clans which may hunt the animal; the clan members concede to these other clans a sort of power over the hunted animal by means of 'hunting couplets'.[241] These formulae also evoke the powers of the totemic species and of the magical charms it provides.[242] From this one could conclude that the Parnkalla tribe were familiar with oral rites of the type practised by the two tribes of Queensland, at such a distance from them as to make any kind of borrowing out of the question. One can even see, in the similarity, evidence for the possibility of a parallel evolution, a common tendency towards the formation of prayers properly so-called.

The principal characteristics of prayer are in fact already there, only in outline certainly, but already imbued with a fairly strong religious sense. Already these rites stand out from Australian ritual in general by virtue of the regularities of the rite and the obligation to perform it in the Mallanpara case,

---

* 'these species'. Here Mauss is probably thinking of the end of note 234.

and by virtue of the divinatory emotion which it confers on those who practice it, and the prophetic quality of the dreams it gives in the Kokowarra* case. Furthermore, they lack none of the general characteristics which we have defined as those of prayer. They have effects, they make use of sacred powers conceived of as intermediaries; they form part of a regular cult in two cases, of an organized cult in the other. However, let us be fully aware of the distance between a rite of this type and the mentality which it reveals, and rites of the higher type. There is a very fine line between invocation and evocation, even magical evocation. Only one invocation, that of the Mallanpara, alludes to that distant place which in developed rituals is the abode of the gods. What it shows with an imperative brevity is 'Where? where?'. It is an invocatory appeal which is a sort of order: the god comes when he is called, as a dog comes at the sound of his master's voice.

We shall find these rites for calling the totem elsewhere. They have their place in other groups of practices, in the most important ceremonies of the Australian cult.[243] We shall dwell more fully on their significance at that point. This will also, in retrospect, enhance the importance of the facts just mentioned.

In all the other Australian practices of totemism, we find only one report which squares fairly well with the idea we usually have of prayer: it is just one among the many formulae addressed to the Wollunqua.[244] This being is a fabulous serpent, the only one of its kind, which, however, gave birth to a clan which bears its name and which differs in no way from the other totemic clans[245] of the Warramunga (central Australia). This prayer was repeated by the two headmen of the clan when they took Spencer and Gillen to Thapauerlu,[246] to the 'water hole'[247] into the cave where the serpent lives. 'They told him that they had brought two important white men to see where he lived; and they asked him not to harm them or us'.[248] They explained to him also that they were his friends and allies. We should note the significance of the fact that an address such as this to a divine being is indeed isolated. According to Spencer and Gillen, the rites of the Wollunqua clan were the only ones of all the tribes they observed that had a propitiatory character.[249] But among these rites, only one formula reflects the general orientation of all these practices, which in any case is still inchoate.[250] What is more, it is a formula which does not even appear to be perfectly integrated into the cult. It is used on a particular occasion and spoken in the presence of white men who were originally initiated, but foreigners all the same. To sum up, the high point reached by these formulae of totemic ritual in their tendency towards other types of prayer, is neither really stable nor very elevated.[251]

There remains the cult of the great spirits or great gods. This also contains certain oral rites in which there is something more than commands, recitals or invocations.

---

* Is Kokowarra a slip or an alternative for the Koko-yimidir of note 234?

In the Pita-Pita tribe of Boulia, it is customary to make brief addresses[252] to Karnmari, the great water serpent, the spirit of nature, initiator of medicine-men. These addresses are exactly similar to the one pronounced by the two headmen of the Wollunqua clan near the home of their direct ancestor. But Karnmari appears to be quite detached from any totem. He appears at the time of torrential floods when he drowns the imprudent. The wise person should speak to Karnmari and say something like this: 'Don't touch me, I belong to this country'. In short, the words spoken here serve to inform the presiding spirit of the locality, to ask his permission to pass through it and to explain to him one's reason for counting on his goodwill. One speaks and asks a favour and the torrent abates. However, we should not exaggerate the quality of this prayer. It conjures up rather than beseeches. It is here more like a password for the people of that region, who are alone the relatives and friends of Karnmari – such is the relationship of the people of the Wollunqua to their totem.[253] It should then be likened to all those permissions asked of local spirits, whether totemic or otherwise.[254] Once personal or impersonal beings become so closely linked with a locality as to become owners of it, it becomes necessary to behave with them as one would with human owners.

But with the Australians the spirits have not all remained as linked to nature as Karnmari or Wollunqua. Many societies, even in the centre and the west,[255] have arrived, in varying degrees, at the notion of the great god, most often a celestial being.[256] The societies even believed in these gods sufficiently strongly to direct a sort of worship towards them, or at least to make them into more or less active witnesses of their rites. One of the most remarkable of these divine beings is Atnatu,[257] the god of initiation[258] in the Kaitish tribe, one of the tribes which Spencer and Gillen deem quite incapable of such a cult.[259] Atnatu was born almost at the beginning of the world and, together with the ancestors of various totems, transformed things which were crude and imperfect into things that were vital and complete. He lives in the sky with his wives, the stars, and with his sons who are also stars, *atnatus* like him. From there, he sees and hears human beings. He listens to see whether they sound the 'devils' of initiation in a proper manner and intone all the appropriate chants correctly.[260] If he does not hear them, he transfixes the impious with his spear and drags them up to the sky. If he hears them, he himself proceeds with the initiation of one of his sons. We do not know the purport of these chants, nor whether they are the chants of various totems or those of the initiation properly so-called; probably it is a question of both. But if their efficacious character is very marked, it is no less certain that they are addressed to a god; that this god is by no means a pale and exoteric mythical figure; and that these chants form part of the ceremonies which the tribesmen used to and still must repeat 'for him'.[261]

In most tribes of New South Wales, and in the north of Victoria and the south of Queensland, initiation rites[262] normally involve the presence of a great god.[263] But this being, who does not seem to be the object of any kind of adoration outside these ceremonies, is at least the recipient of invocations. People call him by his name,[264] they describe what they do for him and what he does;[265] and, as in a litany, evoke him 'by his synonyms'.[266] As Howitt says, 'There is no worship of Daramulun, but the dances around his clay effigy and his invocation by name by the medicine-men could certainly have led to that point'.[267] Other ceremonies include a sort of demonstration which can also be evocatory. It is silent but so expressive that it can really be considered as one of those cases , so frequent with Australians, where religion has used gestures to replace words.[268] In the Bunan (N.-E. Victoria, S.- E. New South Wales, Yuin), the men raise their arms to the sky which signifies 'the Great Lord',[269] the esoteric name for Daramulun. In the same way in the Burbung, in the initiation circle the Wiraijuri tribe make a similar demonstration to their great god.[270]

Practices of this sort seem to be confined to initiation rites which, naturally, are tribal. However, instances can be found elsewhere. In the presence of Taplin, the Narinyerri made a demonstration of this type to the heavens, shouting their invocation and repeating this act several times. At a great Kangaroo round-up, the men chanted in chorus, then rushed holding their spears in front of them towards the smoke of the fire on which a wallaby was cooking. Then they raised their weapons to the sky.[271] The ceremony was founded by Nurundere who is a great god and is addressed to him.[272]

However important these facts may be, they only show us Australian civilizations embarking on the route which leads to prayer made to gods – to great gods. The simplicity of the formulae, almost all reduced to calling out the name of the god, together with the scope of these formulae, which evoke rather than invoke, place them in reality among the other formulae. These we shall encounter in initiation chants, of which they are part or in the chants of the totem cult to which they are juxtaposed. They are attempts, but very rough attempts, to express in the most summary phraseology that the divinity is far off and that one wishes to make the divinity draw near.

It is most remarkable that among the oral rites it should be those of the medicine-men in which we see most clearly the beginnings of what will one day be prayer, that is, when it will have a different appearance from what we can discern in Australia. How can an institution, whose evolution was so important to the development of religion, owe so much to medicine-men? It would be impossible to understand if one did not know from other sources[273] that medicine-men form the intellectual élite of primitive societies and are among the most active agents of their progress. But there are two aspects of their rites, at least such as they generally represent them to ordinary people and among themselves, where they can show elements which, in other civilizations will be typical of all precatory ritual.

On the one hand the magicians are dealing with great gods, from whom they frequently obtain their power. When inspired in the course of their initiation ceremonies, they not only have regular conversations with them[274] but also in some cases they have requests to make to them. So it is in the Anula tribe (Gulf of Carpentaria) that we perhaps find a sort of veritable prayer of petition. There are two evil spirits which inflict illness opposed by a third called by the same name, Gnabaia, who cures illness.[275] The medicine-man 'sings to him[276] to come and cure the sick person'. There must be the same sort of rites among the Binbinga: the medicine-man has two gods, one being the double of the other and also the double, indeed the soul of the medicine-man, who has the same name as the god. It is this second god who has the medical powers and assists at operations. Further, since at a certain moment, the Munkaninji asks the god Munkaninji for permission to show to those present the magic bone, which is the cause of the illness, it is very likely that Munkaninji has been called upon previously and given some idea of the desired result.[277] Is this certain? It seems to us in any case that formulae of this sort are necessary in the rite used by the Binbinga and the Mara, which involves calling on, as with the Anula,[278] a third spirit to counter the two evil initiatory spirits of the medicine-men.[279] The way in which a sacrifice serves to acquire the magic power itself[280] makes us think that the medicine-men of these tribes had already reached or claim to have reached ritual refinements of a fairly high level.

On the other hand, the medicine-men were still meeting beings of a quite individual and sacred nature, with whom they could, and in certain tribes were obliged to converse on a regular basis. These are the dead, from whom they also derive their special powers. Naturally, as by a reversal the medicine-men are superior to their ministering spirits, most of these rites seem to be simple evocations rather than invocations. A good example can be found in the old work of Dawson on the tribes of north-west Victoria. However, not all the formulae are so obviously magical in character. The meaning of certain traditional magical expressions is already less fixed. So Howitt can give three separate translations of the same formula of the Mulla mullung (master of white magic), called Tulaba, interpreting it alternately as supplicatory and evocatory.[281] But other facts are more definite. In time of danger, the Jupagalk of west Victoria would beg a dead friend to come and visit them in a dream and teach them the formulae which counter an evil spell.[282] The Bunurong (Victoria, Melbourne) used to 'entreat' the Len-ba-moor or spirits of the dead to enter the sick part and remove the spell which had caused the illness.[283] This seems likely, especially when compared with the rite of the Anula which we have just mentioned; but the words probably did not have such a clear form of entreaty.

These, then, are the facts which prove that, even in Australia, there are prayers and elements of prayer of a fairly developed kind. We are now in a position to embark on the study of other types of prayer less closely related to the types known to us. For one thing, we can now be sure that the elementary oral rites we are about to describe are indeed those which could have evolved into the rites we have just discussed, because we see the former co-existing with the latter in the same civilization and the same ritual. And we can easily link the first with the prayers of the totemic cult and the second with those of the initiation cult. Within the great mass of living but well used prayers, which are quite unlike anything we normally call by that name, we have seen the birth of nuclei and seeds –the first hint of colour in the centre from which new forms of the institution will eventually emerge.

But we shall have an even better impression of the religious richness of elementary Australian oral ritual when we have analysed each of its components. Despite the distance separating them, the formulae of the totemic and initiation cults will seem to us to have the same generic nature and social function as classic forms of prayer. At the same time in our view, we shall be in a position to attempt an explanation of these elementary forms and have a grasp of their conditions and underlying causes, which are to be found in the mentality of people living in extremely primitive groupings. While the historical analysis of large collections of more advanced prayers would not even have set us on the track of primitive forms, we are already on the path to study the root causes. The way we have chosen leads to this end and helps us to reach conclusions about the evolutionary possibilities within these primitive forms, and about the causes which may have brought about such evolution.

Chapter 3

The Formulae of the Intichiuma

I. Introduction

We have, in fact, yet to describe and analyse a considerable number of oral rites of an obviously religious nature which are, no less obviously, addressed to beings considered as sacred. A terminology steeped in theology would doubtless refuse to call them by the name of prayer; for they are neither the expression of an individual state of soul nor that of a belief or desire. On the contrary, just to transcribe them will be enough to show that they deserve this title, as long as it is broadly interpreted. And the very abundance of data will demonstrate the importance of the barbarous formulae, which form the bulk and centre of gravity of Australian oral ritual.

We shall not study them outside the context of the ceremonies in which they occur. This method, which is so to speak exclusively literary and philological, is only applicable to very advanced types of ritual where prayer is already firmly established in its own right. Even then it is often dangerous to isolate such a study in this way. It can hardly reveal anything except desires expressed, if there are any, the beings invoked, when named, and some of the relationships which the worshippers believe to exist with those beings. But such a study cannot bring out the most intimate of these relationships nor, above all, the manner in which the words are effective. This cannot be appreciated unless, in a rite which is both bodily and oral, one can measure the respective roles given to the two parts of the rite. The efficacy of the word, and the links between a man and his gods – these two essential elements of prayer – are no longer a problem of explanation but become the necessary 'givens' from which one has to start, or the fundamental principles to which one can work backwards.

An example of the dangers of this method can be found in the otherwise very valuable work of Ausfeld on prayer in Greece.[284] Among the questions he neglects – and everyone has the right to neglect some questions – is precisely that of the very meaning of prayer in these religions. Now, having well shown that prayers are above all ritual,[285] had he studied their relation to sacrificial or other rites, he would have been able to determine the general function fulfilled by prayer in the Greek tradition. He could have seen Greek prayer as consisting in little more than a vow or εὐχή[286] and in sum as a means of expressing primarily the bonds established by other rites or by natural qualities between the Greeks and their gods.

It would be even more hazardous to treat prayer in isolation in Australia where it is not, so to speak, an autonomous rite in any sense. It is not self-sufficient. We shall find only a few cases in which it has been sufficiently separated from material actions to seem to have a certain independence. And in one such case[287] the prayer is no longer even in the form of words but is merely an extraordinarily monotonous cry. Most of the time, it is no more than the accompaniment of another rite, however lengthy the periods of time it occupies. Often it is nothing but a sort of emotive frill, a brief expression of violent emotions and poor imagery implied by brutal, painful or passionate acts. So it is impossible here to abstract the spoken word from bodily gestures. Sometimes these gestures occur on their own; always they fill out the true meaning of the oral acts.

So first of all it will be necessary to locate Australian prayers in their ritual background. In order to understand them, we shall have to confine ourselves at first to a review of the documents which give an account of oral rites linked with ceremonial: on the way, we shall try to sift out the elements of prayer that may be found there.

This procedure has the disadvantage of obliging us to repeat ourselves somewhat. These religions are poor in variations, so we shall find identical formulae for ceremonies of differing import and invariable bodily positions accompanying a variety of prayers. In order to avoid repetition, one might be tempted to arrange the facts differently. It would have been tempting, for example, to proceed at once to a classification of prayers according to their nature and modality. But we thought it preferable to proceed more simply and make a complete inventory of the facts without imposing on them, as it were, in advance a ready-made framework. Thus we shall merely set out the oral rites according to the different religious institutions of which they are the essential prayers. By taking on the task of a scrupulous study of *all* the documents, we shall convey the impression that we have conscientiously looked for the facts that contradict our argument without any preconceived systematization. Besides, an immediate classification of the formulae, which would necessarily be rigid, would have excluded from our exposé the description of many links which it is useful for the reader to know. In particular it very often happens that, at the same ceremony, there is a succession of prayers of divergent meaning and different value; to isolate them one from another and to take them out of their context of bodily behaviour, would be impossible and, in any case, would lead to error.

Also, in the course of the description itself, we shall be able to pick out the main types. Taking advantage of the fact that one group of tribes has developed one of them rather than another, we shall be able to assess the similarities and differences while following a historical, geographical, and if you will, ethnographical order. Thus, we shall leave the oral rites *in situ*, in their original setting, and at the same time we shall also be able to classify them.

Among those ceremonies which are certainly basic to Australian religions, we can distinguish three main groups:

1. Totemic ceremonies whose purpose is to act upon the totemic object or species.
2. Totemic ceremonies which form part of initiation rites.
3. Initiation rites properly so-called: circumcision, tooth-avulsion, depilation, etc.

These three groups also form a very well structured system. Around them we can easily group a whole range of scattered related rites and cults pertaining to the marriage classes, to the tribe or to individuals. Also later on, we shall easily be able to show their generic unity and their common origins.

In these three components of Australian religions we find a large number of oral rites.

We call the ceremonies of the first group *intichiuma*. We have kept the name which was borrowed, perhaps inaccurately[288] from the Arunta of central Australia[289] by Spencer and Gillen, who applied it to all the ceremonies of the same type that they noted in the neighbouring tribes to the north and south. In general we regard it as dangerous to extend the name of a custom, which is likely to be peculiar to one people, to a whole series of similar or homologous customs found among other peoples. But within the compass of our science, the name has caught on and, as long as it is clearly defined, we can safely use it.

Intichiuma are those totemic clan ceremonies which have a direct and to a certain extent exclusive effect on the totemic species or object. Such a definition differs considerably from those proposed elsewhere[290] but will be justified by everything that follows. In particular we shall see how mistaken we would be to follow our predecessors in prejudging the magical character of the rites, or in failing to include among the functions of ritual, rites that limit the existence of the totem, as well as those that augment it.[291]

In order to understand the ritual of the Australian intichiuma, we shall first of all study the intichiumas of the Arunta in their entirety. These are the ones that were first known to us as such and are the best known to us. Since they comprise not only a large number of oral rites, whose import is fairly clear and whose text is well established, together with nearly all the variations thereof, they provide an excellent starting-point. We should add that for the Arunta we have a better knowledge than for any other tribe of the ritual, mythological and social conditions in which these formulae repeatedly appear. We shall go on to describe the intichiuma of the Warramunga, which will show us a unique type of oral rites which by themselves comprise practically the entire intichiuma ritual of this tribe. Around these two central Australian tribes we shall group the tribes which inhabit the rest of Australia, whose organization and civilization are very different; we shall show that they, too, possess this religious institution in more or less developed form and that it comprises in its turn equivalent forms of prayer used under equivalent conditions.

II. The intichiumas of the Arunta

The Arunta are at present the best known tribe in Australia.[292] They inhabit the enormous territory from 132° East of Greenwich to 136° longitude and more than three degrees latitude, 23° to 26°. They are one of the most powerful tribes to have inhabited Australia.[293] Numbering more than 1,200, they comprise more than a hundred local totemic groups. Perhaps they are more of a confederation than a single tribe.[294] We are led to this conclusion by certain important variations in dialect,[295] in rituals such as initiation,[296] in social organization[297] and by the fact that at least one part of the tribe (living by the River Finke) seems to enjoy a completely separate organization.[298] They do not by any means live in the completely desolate country which some descriptions would lead us to believe.[299] The country where they roam is steppe interspersed with dunes and patches of rock but there is a fairly good water supply. Although the rivers no longer empty themselves as far as Lake Eyre, they are full of fish and never run dry. Wide, deep valleys provide well-stocked hunting-grounds and the small oases of the desert and steppe make excellent reservations.[300] So, despite their primitive technology,[301] the Arunta, like the majority of Australian tribes in general, were able to support themselves by happily adapting to a favourable environment. Their economy left them with sufficient leisure and gave them no urge towards technical or scientific progress.[302] Whole months were taken up with tribal or even inter-tribal gatherings, devoted to long initiation festivities[303] in which simple feasts and celebrations were mingled with the most sacred rites. All this presupposes soil that was abundant in grain, reptiles and insects, as well as good hunting and a certain accumulation of provisions.

Under these material conditions, the Arunta developed an extremely elaborate social organization which has probably since been allowed to degenerate.[304] The whole tribe is divided into two phratries; formerly, and still in principle today, the totems were shared out between them.[305] These two phratries were themselves divided into a total of four or eight matrimonial classes according to whether one was in the south, south-west or north of the tribe.[306] These classes enable one to take account both of the position of the totemic clans within the phratries, and of matrilineal and patrilineal descent.[307] At least, they fulfilled this function until, for unknown reasons, totemic inheritance, which must have operated extremely regularly for a long time,[308] as it did among all the neighbours of the Arunta,[309] ceased to operate in a non-miraculous manner.

But from the point of view of the totemic cult, we should note the importance and the considerable number of totemic clans. Spencer and Gillen list at least 62 in their first work[310] and 75 in the list they give in their second book.[311] From the myths collected by Strehlow and which, according to him, concern solely totemic gods,[312] we can make a list of more than 99 totems, excluding a great number of sub-totems. This would mean an average of about 10 individuals per totemic clan; and since some clans have a large number of members while others have only a few, or even only one,[313] and since as from the special point of view of the intichiumas each clan has its own,[314] one can see the extreme complexity of the cult. Finally, since in a large clan, each local group has its own intichiuma[315] and there can be several intichiumas per clan,[316] it is reasonable to suppose that we know only a very small part of the ritual. Out of these more than 150 intichiumas, there are scarcely 15 for which we have the formulae and rites. But, in spite of an extreme variety of specialized forms, this ritual, as we shall see, is extremely uniform.[317] Moreover, however numerous the clans may be, they are in such close relations with each other that they form a very well organized religious society. From the intichiuma we know, we can form certain safe conclusions about those we do not know, or those we know only by induction[318] or by their myths.[319]

The most ancient detailed document on the Arunta gives us an excellent description of the intichiuma and its formulae, its feasts and *tjurunga* songs as Schulze called them[320] or, as he translated, their 'prayers for foodstuffs'.[321] He even gave the name intichiuma to all the ceremonies of the totemic cult which he considered related 'exclusively to food' and to the means of acquiring it.[322] From that time, the nature of the songs and the ritual conditions under which they were repeated, were known.

In the first place, Schulze showed quite clearly the religious nature of the ceremony.[323] Then he noted carefully that in its totality, including the formula, the ritual objects and gestures, it was the property, not of a private individual but of a sort of priest acting on behalf of the clan and for the society as a whole, that is, all the other clans.[324] Finally, he established as a general rule that, whatever the pre-eminence of the headman to whom the ceremony belonged, it nevertheless had a collective character and presupposed an audience which would take an active part in the ceremony by singing, if not by dancing, which was delegated to actors.[325]

We have firmly established the nature of the ceremony and the religious conditions of an essentially practical and collective nature, under which the formulae are repeated. Now we turn to the formula itself.

Firstly, it is definitely musical, rhythmic and methodical:[326] it is a song. This song either serves as an accompaniment to the dance of an actor or a small group of mimes or else, having accompanied the mimed dance and thus fulfilled its function, it continues indefinitely at the same more or less rapid rhythm, with the same tune transposed at the most up or down an octave or a fifth.[327] This song is closely linked to the bodily rite, to which it is subordinated, its only function being to impart the dance rhythm and shape; so it continues, like a stereotyped gesture, until the dancer has stopped, exhausted. Furthermore, according to Schulze, we can infer that the continued beating of time with the *tnuma* or tapping-sticks, constitutes at least a ritual gesture. The rhythm and metre of the formula spring from the dramatic purpose of the exercise.

But sometimes the oral rite can be nothing more than a simple cry,[328] the cry of the animal being represented;[329] we have already seen examples of this custom in the calls addressed to the totem. In this case, it is even more clearly a mere gesture, a rhythmic sound, either imitating, as here, the natural rhythm of a bird song,[330] or repeated at regular intervals, separated by pauses, with a single steady beat. It is most remarkable that Spencer and Gillen should have failed to mention the role of this cry in the Arunta ceremonies.[331]

The cry is necessarily monotonous. It is repeated indefinitely: it ends by being a sort of vocal habit.[332] Even the modulation ceases to be free: variations are impossible. So the cry is scarcely more than a gesture, one more way of miming the animal. It is no more than the vocal trimming on the action.

But one should not exaggerate the distance between the cry and the formula, for the latter is hardly longer than a cry. Its musical value and length vary only slightly. The step of the dance is itself so monotonous that it imposes a certain monotony. And when the song ceases to be danced, it does not change in form, rhythm, tune or bottom-line. Repetition is essential to the *tjurunga* chant, according to Schulze, as it is to the cry.[333]

It is unfortunate that the German missionary did not give a complete description of a particular intichiuma but confined himself to a general description and an indication of the orientation of the rites. For him, it is no more than a mime accompanied by a song.[334] But at least he gives us valuable details about the formulae and their meaning.

Firstly and correctly, he notes their simplicity. He believes that they only consist of four or five words arranged according to the poor syntax of these languages and rarely change.[335] And even when the fact is not immediately apparent, they only express a wish[336] or a prayer. One of the formulae he cites calls to mind precisely the sort of cries that we, on the basis of mere prejudice, are accustomed to associate with savages. Here it is:

Galbmantalanta	*janiau*	*gatitjalanta*	*janiau*
Honey much	yes yes	much much	yes yes[337]

Although this sentence can have many meanings,[338] certainly its chief characteristic is the blunt expression by means of simple nouns, pronouns, adverbs and interjections, of an extraordinarily intense desire and also an anticipated satisfaction of that desire. A child shows the same attitude when he sees the thing he wants: the anticipated satisfaction makes the object as real to him as if he already possessed it. In short, not only the desire but also the moral effect of the rite are immediately felt and expressed. The other formulae cited and translated by Schulze would not be as clear without his commentary. One of them seems merely to be an aphoristic summary, or a sort of musical title of a myth: it is the *tjurunga* of the bird *Lambulambila.*

Lambulambila laintjirbmana
The (name of the bird) is on the water which is on the mountain[339]

The two others, which form part of the *tjurunga* of the feast of the emu, express the present existence of something from the past, but from a very recent and altogether concrete past, like the tracks found by a hunter. They describe the trail of the game, that is, a place where the animal has just been, which it has just left, a point from which one can sense its existence, a path on which one is certain to catch up with it.

Tijatitjana jala ramana
Great emus many tracks[340]
Magatjagatjana werilankana
Innumerable emus have been here[341]

The two lines obviously correspond. Not only their continual repetition but also their metric break and their balance makes for a rhythmic effect. Schulze said of them,[342]

> All the festivals refer exclusively to eating or to the supply of food, and it is pointed out whence the various objects as emu, fishes, &c., are derived; in what number and size they formerly existed, &c., which forms also the burden of their songs. These festivals serve as reminders, and extol the past, conjoined with prayers that these animals, &c., may again appear in the same numbers, of similar size, &c.

There is a constant, easy and immediate passage from the mythical past to the ritual future. The actual moment of the intichiuma, the formula which goes with the dance or the rite, is such that one passes imperceptibly from the simple description of the past or present to an instantly effective wish, to the demonstration of the desired result as if it too had already been granted.

A final characteristic of the formulae, according to Schulze, is their obscurity and unintelligibility.[343] Nearly everyone in the tribe is ignorant of their meaning, with the exception at least of their 'owner'.[344] The language in which they are couched is not the profane language of the women, children and men of the camp; most of the time, it consists of obsolete and archaic words 'partly taken from other dialects'. Schulze gives the reason for this concisely: it is that they are 'derived from their ancestors'.[345] Naturally, the ancestors, being superhuman and foreign to their descendants, spoke a different language from them. So a new detail is added to our picture: the language of the formulae is distinct from the vulgar, everyday language. These formulae were used by the ancestors themselves and the prayers and phrases addressed to them are spoken in their own language.

We can find nothing to reject in Schulze's analysis made many years ago. We are now in a position to indicate the general characteristics, not only of the intichiuma formulae, but also of all the rest of the Australian religious ritual.

All the formulae we shall meet henceforth are the following:

I. WITH REGARD TO THE RITUAL FORMULA

1. *musical*, that is, *melodic and rhythmic*;
2. *give directions* for gestures, mimes or dances;
3. *sung collectively*;
4. *repeated in a monotonous way*, even when they are independent of the dance.[346]

II. WITH REGARD TO THE LITERARY STRUCTURE OF THE FORMULAE

1. *simple, being sometimes only a cry or a short phrase*;
2. *eminently descriptive*, either of a past which blends with the present or future, or rather of the desired result;
3. *usually composed and performed in language that is not understood* by the public uninitiated to the hidden knowledge of the rite;
4. finally, by their intrinsic value as much as by their relationship to the ceremony of which they are part, they are *efficacious*, in the way we have claimed applies to prayer, understood in a very broad sense.

All the characteristics of this picture apply to all the oral rites of the totemic or tribal cult which we shall describe in this chapter and the two following. We shall note the rare apparent exceptions and we know of no real exceptions to the rules we have just laid down. We shall not return to this rule, despite the considerable role we shall have to give it later on [Book III] in our attempts at explanation.

All we can see at present is how far we are from mental and personal prayer. There is nothing here except the practical, immediate and concrete – nothing that fails to correspond to a material need; nothing here but what is collective, banal, stereotyped and mechanical. If primitive prayer had been no more than this, how could other forms of prayer have grown out of it? It must have contained other elements which we were forced to neglect because of the poverty of Schulze's documentation. Underneath the outer covering of ritual conditions and verbal forms, there must have been other beliefs and other feelings, something more than the brute force of the words. Spencer and Gillen's more detailed descriptions on the one hand, and Strehlow's on the other, will give us some idea of this. At the same time we shall be able to detect the formation of different varieties* of prayers. We shall see the appearance of different types and we shall be able to catch a glimpse of the way in which they will develop.

As for general characteristics of the intichiuma,[347] Spencer and Gillen add only two to those described by Schulze.

1. As well as being the exclusive property of the clan, they are also, for the most part, its secret. They cannot even be watched by spectators other than the members of the clan, or of the phratry to which the clan is more particularly linked. Here Spencer and Gillen flatly contradict Schulze, who made no distinction between intichiumas and the sacred ceremonies or the *tjurunga* of the totems, and did not specify this ritual condition.[348]
2. Then, they are perfectly regular and being annual are repeated at each season.[349]

But let us pass over these two characteristics. They are almost peculiar to the intichiumas of the Arunta. On the other hand, a certain number of characteristics, which are common in some degree to the most diverse intichiumas, will help us to complete the general description of the formulae and their value which we have just attempted.

To facilitate our explanation and also because such a division corresponds with the facts, we shall divide these ceremonies into three groups according to the types of formulae employed. The first are intichiumas with formulae; the second are intichiumas with hymns; finally the rest, the largest group, from the point of view of the forms they use, consist of a mixture of the other two types.

I. The formula

One of the most advanced intichiumas we know is that of the *witchetty grub clan*,[350] and within this clan that of the Alice Springs group,[351] which is the largest of all the divisions of the tribe.[352] What is more, we know not only the oral and bodily rites[353] but also the myth.[354] The only real gap in our knowledge is that we still do not know the text of the formulae used: we know only the meaning.

---

* French, *espèces*, like *genres*, still has for Mauss some biological, scientific connotations. Translated here as varieties.

Led by the *alatunja,*[355] that is, the headman of the local totemic group, the owner and controller of ceremony, the people of the totem leave the camp in secret and in silence, absolutely naked, and without implements of any kind. They will not eat until the end of the ceremony.[356] In this way they come to Emily Gorge, the mythical centre of the totem, the principal residence of the bodies and souls of the ancestors, the foetal souls and seeds of men and beasts which are ready to be incarnated in the bodies of female butterflies and of women.[357] They spend the night there.[358] The next day, they leave, holding branches of gum tree in their hands, the *alatunja*[359] carrying nothing but a small wooden bowl, such as the great ancestor possessed.[360] And they will follow the tracks left by the leader of the grubs which founded the camp, Intwailiuka, who was born, or rather came into the world, at the north of this gorge.[361] In the same way, a pilgrimage directs a procession to the various places where a saint is commemorated. At the end of this journey through the world of myth, they come to a vast cavern, a hole[362] where a huge block of quartzite stands surrounded by round stones. The quartzite represents the *maegwa*, the adult insect.[363] The *alatunja* begins to chant, striking the stone with his *apmara* or small bowl. And the others take up the chant, striking the rock with their branches[364] and singing the chant, which has the refrain of inviting the animal to lay its eggs.[365] This goes on for some time. Then, in the same way and probably with the same chants, they strike the small stones which represent the eggs which the ancestors (men-grubs) once carried.[366] Intiwailiuka had done all this, at the same place on the same stones, because he also had performed the intichiuma.[367] Then they come to *Alknalinta*, the rock with eyes,[368] at the foot of which there is another adult stone-insect or *maegwa churinga*, buried deep in the sand. The *alatunja* again strikes the rock with his apmara. The others follow suit again with their branches, 'while the old men repeat a lively sung invitation: that the insects may come from all directions and lay their eggs'.[369] Intiwailiuka also amused himself at this place by throwing the sacred churinga eggs in the air along the length of the rock; and they would roll back to his feet. The *alatunja* imitates this act with the *churinga* stones which are both the ancestor's eggs and the present-day symbols of the individual souls, human and animal, past, present and future.[370] During this rite the other members of the clan go up and down the whole length of the rock wall 'chanting continuously, we do not know what, but evidently a phrase describing this act performed by the ancestor.' The first act of the liturgy is ended. Incantation has been made to the adult insect, it has laid its eggs. There is a change of scene and subject. They turn back to the camp.[371]

They continue to follow the story of the animal species, which is both mythical and natural, both curiously imaginative and realistic. Now they concentrate on the larva and the chrysalis. They proceed on the homeward journey, like grubs, which progress slowly, stopping in succession at some ten holes or *ilthura*, simple hollows containing large stones, covered with sand and soil, one or two stones in each hole. They are unearthed and represent the chrysalides or the eggs of the insect.[372] While he lifts out each of these sacred objects, the *alatunja* 'sings a monotonous chant concerning the chrysalis.' When they are exposed, 'songs are sung[373] about the *uchaqua*' (the name of the chrysalis and of this sacred stone). They are rubbed one by one; the men pick them up and anoint them because they are relics to be venerated, and will produce grubs, insects and eggs. The ceremony is repeated at each of the ten *ilthura* or stations of these pious pilgrims.[374] These chants are the ones once sung by the ancestor, the head of the clan, and heard by other ancestors of the same totem in another locality.[375]

The third and final act is the return to the camp. The men decorate themselves, the *alatunja* less than the others. Each man has painted on his body the sacred design or emblem which identifies people with their totems – that is, each individual with the ancestor whom he reincarnates and who, as both man and beast, once bore the same emblem.[376] This time, all of them carry branches of bushes; they wave them constantly as they walk in single file.[377] While they were away on their mystical expedition, one of the old men had built away from the camp, a long narrow hut made of branches called the *umbana*, which is the name of the chrysalis and which seems to us rather to represent the cocoon. All the local people are there, including the women, with different decorations.[378] As soon as the old man see the troupe of ritual actors in the distance, he starts to sing a formula whose meaning is unknown to us.

Ilkna pung kwai
Yaalan nik nai,
Yu mulk la
Naantai yaa lai[379]

The troupe draws near and in the same way as Intwailiuka used to stop to look at women, so the *alatunja* stops and runs his eye over them. Then they all go into the *umbana*. 'And then they all start to chant, singing about the animal in its various states, the *Alknalinta* stone and the great *maegwa* at its base.[380] The men and women of the other phratry are lined up there, lying face down: they must not move or speak a word during the entire rite. The singing continues. Meanwhile the *alatunja* comes out of the *umbana*, crawling and sliding by imperceptible degrees along the prepared stretch of earth. All the men imitate him and, once they are all outside, they sing the story of the *maegwa*, and above all of its covering, the *umbana*.[381] Then they creep back inside in the same way and the singing stops. It is at this point that they may eat and drink for the first time for many hours.[382]

We can consider the very last rite of this series as a sort of epilogue. But it is not the least interesting since it is in fact given over to chants, to oral rites whose efficacy is particularly apparent. All night the clan members remain seated on the other side of the *umbana* in front of a big fire 'singing the witchetty grub'. They cannot be seen by the other phratry who remain prostrate. Then suddenly at sunrise the chant stops, the camp fire is put out by the *alatunja* and the members of the other phratry are free to move.[383] After this come the sacramental rites of the totem and the exit rites which we need not consider here.[384]

One can see straight away that these oral rites all correspond to the general type we have established. They are monotonous rhythmic chants attached to bodily rites (dances or collective gestures),[385] although sometimes they are detached and function autonomously but with no change in rhythm. Only two of them consist of a solo by the headman to which a sort of choir responds.[386] They contain sentiments and ideas that are in no way individual, but merely crude and stark expressions of needs and expectations. What is more, all but two or three of these rites are strictly confined to formulae. Either they give orders to the totemic animal[387] or they give descriptions in a few sober phrases equally applicable to the present, as to the future or the past – eternal as the actions of an animal species. Finally, it is hard to imagine any activity more forcefully obstinate than this endless repetition for forty-eight hours[388] of unpoetical sentences, of uniform musical themes, in short, of chants which are of little artistic merit and quite without appeal to the emotions. Ethnographic reality here presents us with a ritual in which formulae play such a lengthy and systematic role that the boldest hypotheses would hardly have led us to postulate anything comparable. That is why, although it contains two or three formulae which do not belong exclusively to this type,[389] we thought fit to choose it as representative of religious formulae.

But a detailed analysis will reveal other elements than those we have mentioned so far. In fact we can distinguish, beside the characteristics already given, five ritual themes which run through this apparently formless mass of short magico-religious ballads. This makes it into an incomparably rich breviary, despite its simple exterior.

1. As Schulze pointed out,[390] the precatory character of the rite is pronounced. We find an appeal to the divine animal or totem under its different aspects: the insects are called to come and lay their eggs; chants are addressed to the eggs to produce grubs, to the grubs to make cocoons, to the chrysalides to change into butterflies.[391] The totemic species is not simply conceived of as an inert and passive thing; it is a composite of individuals which will converge from all sides when a summons or invitation is made, analogous to one addressed to human beings, inciting it to satisfy the desires of the clan, which acts as interpreter for the whole tribe. In other *intichiumas*, when the totem is simply called by its name without other circumlocutions, as one would hail a fellow human, or when members of a totem simply utter its call, the effect produced on the animal is the same as that attributed to the cry of an animal or the song of a bird to members of its own species.[392]

2. This summons is not conceived of as a prayer which the totem can refuse to answer.[393] It is a kind of order, an imperative suggestion to which it must conform. The season has come for the witchetty grubs to hatch and allow themselves to be eaten[394] by all the faithful Arunta, some of whom, as members of the witchetty grub clan, are their parents and relatives and will not eat them except during the totemic sacrament.[395] Like the first grubs who obeyed the orders of their leader, and like their present-day totemic brothers, the grubs resign themselves to doing as they are told, so they come out, lay eggs and change regularly into butterflies as they see men doing in their ritual drama.[396] Even when they are not expressed in the form of an order, the formulae take the place of a sacramentary injunction.[397]

But as well as such data which are so to speak intrinsic elements in the actual text of the formulae, there are other elements that are equally necessary and that can only be discovered as one studies the relation between formula and myth.

3. In the first place, these formulae are not usually couched in the language of everyday conversation. They possess an authority beyond even the magical powers of the living persons who pronounce them. For such magic power is always feeble, inferior indeed to the mysterious whims and secret understandings which motivate animals and preside over the unstable destinies of things.[398] So the chant is not straightforwardly merely the expression of the wishes of the ritual actors performing on behalf of the tribe, making known their 'will'. It is of higher origin, possesses greater inner power, greater effectiveness and dignity. The words are those used by the ancestral chief and repeated by the other originators of the totem, when the group of witchetty grubs, in the legendary time when men and beasts were one, journeyed, laying their eggs[399] and the *churinga* – the receptacles of the souls of the dead, of the souls of children and the substances of animals.[400] They have a mythical value because they were used at the very origin of the species: it is they who caused the souls of animals and men to be born. They have a value tested by experience because the time, simultaneously infinite and measured historically,[401] which has passed since that legendary age, has seen their efficacy confirmed each season with the birth of the grubs.

As Schulze understood so well, this is the reason which has given rise, as it were to a corollary, to the very form of the formula which is most often incomprehensible, if not to its owners, at least to the tribe at large. It is not composed in everyday language; the mystical rigmarole in which it is spoken is the extraordinary, strange, foreign language of the ancestral founders of the clan.[402] Whether some of the formulae are taken ready-made from a foreign tribe or are composed of ordinary words, distorted so as to become unrecognisble,[403] or whether they are really spoken in a language which is archaic or inaccurately transmitted,[404] they are believed to come from the *Alcheringa* [Dreamtime], from the ancestors of the *Alcheringa*. Their prodigious strength is that which they possessed in the past; but it is only their Sybilline form which makes them all-powerful.

4. But these formulae are not repeated indifferently nor in every place. They are sung only before or over the *churinga* in the sacred places,[405] over the whole set of sacred stones* and over each one individually.[406] So they consist, strictly speaking, of incantations. They cast a spell on and breathe life into these apparently inanimate stones. These blessings, acts of praise and chants make these stones into living beings – eggs, chysalides, grubs and butterflies. The everlasting quality of the stone is complicated by the power of breath, sound and voice.[407] The formula is a means of reviving the mythical ancestors who live in the stones. What is more, as the successive metamorphoses of the animal are linked to its reproduction, through phenomena that are well known to the Arunta, one can understand that such descriptions of the mythical vicissitudes of the species, and these exhortations to reproduce them, have the effect of encouraging the bodies and souls of the *churinga* to multiply the grubs, which is the whole purpose of the rite. In the same way as erotic songs act on human desires, so the formulae prompt beings, animals, men and gods, revitalized by the spoken words of the rite, to the prosperous fulfilment of their destiny.

In the Arunta tribe, according to Strehlow, the rites act upon the *churinga* in the following way.[408] In the depths of the earth, in the great caves or *kalpara*[409] live the *erintaringa*[410] or, as they are called in the tribe of the West,[411] the invisible ones, the *iwopata* who are red all over like the *churinga* anointed with blood or painted with red ochre. These are the *rella ngantja*, the men of the earth;[412] they are the permanent souls of the totemic species, the principle of all fruitfulness. They come out from their underground lairs by night,[413] to reach the surface,to handle and to look at the *tjurunga* where they once lived. With their magic weapons they hunt game on the surface of the earth and take it back underground where they eat it raw. It is these *rella ngantja* that are obliged by the incantation to come up and enter the *churinga*, the stones which produce rain,[414] eggs, insects or animals, stones which are unearthed, handled and anointed. The formula is part of a process of magic. It is magic itself. It unites the bodies and spirits of the divine species and prompts these animated bodies, these ancestors resurrected in all their fabulous strength, to participate in the actions performed in their presence and to propagate the animal species as they have previously done in mythical times.[415] The mode of efficacy is so strong as we have just described it, that in certain cases, probably when the animals appear out of season, Spencer and Gillen tell us that the *iruntarinia*† have performed intichiuma on behalf of men.[416] They have done of their own free will what they normally do only in response to incantation.

---

* French text reads *prières* – surely a misprint for *pierres*.

† This must be the same as *erintaringa* at the beginning of the paragraph.

Notes

Edited by Robert Parkin

The footnotes which Mauss provided for *La Prière* are often inaccurate and sometimes apparently completely spurious. One can only assume that he left them while working on the text, with a view to correcting them later for publication but failed then to do so. An attempt has been made to check them for this English edition, using principally the resources of the Bodleian Library and other libraries in Oxford, and elsewhere. Not even their copious resources, however, have proved sufficient to uncover all the errors and omissions that Mauss left behind. Minor errors and omissions have been corrected discretely when errors by Mauss are certain, but in the case of the more substantial ones an explanatory comment has been provided. The latter have been placed in square brackets and generally signed R. P. Certain footnotes remain inexplicable. Where there are uncertainties, Mauss's notes remain unchanged. Certain details have been added. There are many references of the form: Book II. Chapter I, sometimes followed by the name of a subject. These refer to relevant places in Mauss's thesis. Books I and II of the thesis are presented here. References to Book III relate to further parts of the thesis that have never been found. Beyond what was published, they indicate that Mauss had carefully planned much, if not all, the thesis.

1. On these phenomena of transmutation in art and in what he calls 'myth', see the ingenious observations of W. Wundt on the 'Umwandlung der Motive', *Völkerpsychologie*, Leipzig, 1900–20, II, I, pp. 430, 590.
2. On the relationship between myth and ritual, see our observations in *L'Année sociologique*, II; VI, Introduction *Les Mythes* (rubric), pp. 243–6; cf. M. Mauss, 'L'art et le mythe d'après M. Wundt', *Revue philosophique de la France et de l'étranger*, LXVI, 1908, p. 17.

3. For an exposition of the ritualist thesis, see R. Smith, *The Religion of the Semites*, 2nd edn., London, 1894, p. 16.
4. In its theoretical form, of course, for Islam has retained sacrifices, most of them being vestiges of ancient cults, in the cult of the saints, the taking of oaths and a good number of more or less popular feasts.
5. See A. Sabatier, *Esquisse d'une philosophie de la religion, d'après la psychologie et l'histoire*, Paris, 1897, p. 24ff.
6. In our view, these general remarks on the evolution of religions are a more accurate version of those elaborated by C.D. Tiele; see *Elements of the Science of Religion*, Edinburgh, 1898, II, p. 130ff.
7. *Jure pontificum cautum est, ne suis nominibus dii Romani appellarentur, ne exaugurari possent*, Servius, *ad Aen.* II, 35 n.; cf. Pliny, N.H. XXVIII, 18; G. O. A. Wissowa, *Religion und Kultus der Römer*, Munich, 1902, p. 333.
8. Part of this history has been described by H. Oldenberg, *Le Boudha, sa vie, sa doctrine, son Eglise*, transl. A. C. A. Foucher, 2nd edn., pp. 1–80 [also transl. W. Hoey, London, 1882. R. P.]; by P. Deussen, *Allgemeine Geschichte der Philosophie*, Vols I and II, Leipzig, 1894–1917; *Die Philosophie des Veda; Die Philosophie der Upanishads*, Berlin, 1896, 1898; by P. [?] Oltramare, *Histoire de la théosophie hindoue, I, Bibl. d'Et. du Musée Guimet.*
9. We are referring primarily to the birth of the synagogue, which is, above all, a prayer 'meeting': see I. Loeb, 'La communauté des pauvres', *Revue des études juives*, 1889; I. Lévi, 'Les dix-huit bénédictions', ibid., 1896, pp. 16, 61; E. Schürer, *Geschichte des Volkes Israel im Zeitalter Jesu Christi*, Leipzig, 2nd edn., 1890, II, p. 45ff. On the origins of Christian prayer, see E. von der Goltz, *Das Gebet in der ältesten Christenheit*, Leipzig, 1901, and our observations, *L'Année sociologique*, VI, p. 216. [Mauss's review of Goltz, pp. 211–17. R. P.]
10. We now know that the Psalms were originally liturgical compositions. Some belong to the temple ritual: the acrostic Psalms of the twelve and twenty-four apostles; cf. H. Gressmann, *Musik und Musikinstrumente im Alten Testament*, Giessen, 1903, the Psalms of the Hallel; cf. T. K. Cheyne, *The Origin and Religious Content of the Psalter*, London 1891. The rest come from the 'community of the poor'; cf. F. Coblentz, *Ueber das betende Ich der Psalmen* etc. Frankfurt, 1897.
11. This is the case, for example, of prayers that have become part of magic; see A. v. Dietrich, *Eine Mithrasliturgie*, [Leipzig? R. P.], 1902.
12. We shall see later that the phenomenon of 'wear and tear' is far from being incompatible with extremely primitive stages of civilization, and we shall find numerous examples in Australia. Book III, Part 2, Chapter III. [For such references, see Parkin above.]
13. On the importance of, for example, this last type of regression in our own countries, one might usefully consult R. Andree, *Ueber Votiv- und Weihegaben*, Brunswick, 1906, where lists of formulae may be found.

14. See below.
15. Cf. below, Book II, Chapter I. See L. Farnell, *Evolution of Religion*, London, 1905, p. 168ff.
16. There is, however, a fine article by A. Kuhn on magic formulae in European folklore: *Zeitschrift für Völkerpsychologie und Sprachwissenschaft*, 1864, XIII, p. 49ff.; p. 113ff. [not found. R. P.]
17. See below, the discussion of a short work by Max Müller, actually a résumé of an Oxford University course.
18. Towards the end of their lives, however, H. K. Usener (cf. 'Ueber zwei Rechtsriten', *Hessische Blätter für Volkskunde*, I, 1902) and V. Henry (*Magic in Ancient India* [also *La magie dans l'Inde*, Paris, 1904, 2nd edn. 1909, R. P.]) showed a growing interest in the study of rites as such.
19. Cf. also J.G. Frazer, *On the Scope of Social Anthropology*, inaugural lecture, London, 1908.
20. Cf. below, Book II, Chapters I, II.
21. On the subject of prayer among ancient peoples, and for an idea of the ignorance which still exists about these questions as regards Greece and Rome, see C. Ausfeld, 'De graecorum precationibus quaestiones', *Jahrbuch für Klassische Philosophie*, Fleckeisen, XXVIII, Teubner, 1903, p. 305ff.; Chételat, *De precatione apud poetas graecos et latinos*, 1877, should also be noted; also L'Abbé Vincent, *La Prière chez les Grecs et les Latins*, 1887; C. Ziegler, *De precationum apud Graecos formis*, etc. Breslau, 1905, dissertation; H. Schmidt, 'Veteres philosophi quomodo judicaverint de praecibus' (*Religionsgeschtliche Untersuchungen und Vorarbeiten*, ed. v. Dietrich and R. Wünsch, IV, I, X, 1907). It is still worth consulting the older work of E. v. Lasaulx, *Die Gebete der Griechen und der Römer*, 1842. But the philologists can scarcely be blamed here: classical literature and even monuments are such a poor source of prayers!
22. The debates on the relative age of the ritual of the Atharva-Veda magicians and the *sutra* that belong to it, together with the rituals of the various priests, Rigveda, Yajurveda, etc., are dominated precisely by questions of this type. Some scholars maintain that the age of the texts is definitely not that of the rituals (*faits*) themselves and that the Atharvavedic tradition is as ancient as the other, while other scholars imply that the numerous borrowings by the Atharva-Veda from other Vedas proves that it is of later date. For an excellent discussion of the question, see M. Bloomfield, *The Atharva Veda*, Strasbourg, 1899 (Grundriss der indo-arischen Philologie), II, I, II.
23. We quote, almost as an exception, the beautiful Pawnee ritual published by Mrs A. Fletcher, 'The Hako: A Pawnee Ceremony', 22nd *Annual Report of the Bureau of American Ethnology*, 1904, I (text, music, theological commentary on the prayers).

24. A. Bergaigne, *La Religion védique d'après les hymnes du Rig-veda*, Paris, 1878–97, II, 2.
25. A. F. Weber, *Indische Studien*, Berlin, 1850–98; H. Oldenberg, *Die Hymnen des Rig Veda*, Berlin, 1888; A. Bergaigne, 'Recherches sur l'histoire de la liturgie védique', *Journal Asiatique*, 8th series, XX, 1892 [actually XIII, 1889, pp. 5–32, 121–97. R. P.]. A good exposé of these questions and their bibliography may be found in M. Winternitz, *Geschichte der indischen Litteratur*, I, Leipzig, 1905, p. 61ff.
26. Sylvain Lévi, *La Doctrine du sacrifice dans les Brahmanes*, Paris, 1898, p. 100.
27. O. Strauss, *Brhaspati im Veda*, dissertation, Kiel, 1905.
28. Cf. above; cf. T. Engert, *Der betende Gerechte der Psalmen*, Würzburg, 1902; O. Dibelius, *Das Vaterunser*, etc., Giessen, 1903 (cf. *L'Année sociologique*, VII, p. 304ff. [Mauss's review of Dibelius. R. P.]).
29. H. Schmidt, *Veteres philosophi*, etc., Giessen, 1907.
30. See J. Jastrow, *The Religion of Babylonia and Assyria*, Boston, 1898, p. 292ff.; F. D. H. Zimmern, *Babylonische Busspsalmen*, Leipzig, 1885; see also the bibliography of the subject in J. Jastrow, *Die assyrisch–babylonische Religion*.
31. L. W. King, *Babylonian Magic and Sorcery*, London, 1896, part I; C. Fossey, *La magie assyrienne*, Paris, 1902, p. 93ff.
32. We cannot quote any general work on prayer in Egypt: the question has been approached only indirectly in philological works, with special reference to the *Book of the Dead*, and in studies of special rituals. The most informative is G. Maspero, 'La Table d'offrandes des tombeaux égyptiens', *Revue de l'histoire des religions*, XXXV, 1897, p. 275–330, XXXVI, 1897, pp. 1–20.
33. Among the very best discussions of this subject is Origen's *De oratione*.
34. For example, the classification of the Vedas into *vedas* of hymns chanted by the *hotar* and sung by the *udgatar* (*Rig-Veda* and *Sama-Veda*); the Veda of formulae murmured or spoken by the *adhvaryu* or officiant (*Yajur Veda*); the *Veda* of magic formulae, of the Brahman (*Atharva Veda*) is really perfect.
35. This is partly why one must understand the history of the dogmatic debates on the canon of the mass or the Psalms. A good exposition of the history of the first debates about the value of the Psalms may be found in Engert [note 28 R.P.]
36. See below.
37. *Elements of the Science of Religion* (Gifford Lectures), 2 vols., Edinburgh, 1898 and 1899. In these lectures, Tiele first discussed the global evolution of religions (animism, polytheism etc.), then the principal institutions (prayer, sacrifice, church, etc.).
38. Tiele, op. cit., II, p. 130; cf. O. Pfleiderer, *Grundriss der Religionsphilosophie*, 2nd edn., Berlin, 1883, p. 301.

39. One could even say this of Protestantism, be it ultra liberal, Socianism or Remonstrant. Tiele was a Remonstrant.
40. Tiele does not say which theorists he disagrees with. We assume that he is referring to Max Müller: see below [n.83].
41. Tiele, op cit., II, p. 133.
42. *Esquisse d'une philosophie de la religion d'après la psychologie et l'histoire*, Paris, 1897, pp. 24, 14.
43. Op. cit., I, Chapter IV, § 4.
44. Op. cit., p. 191.
45. See below.
46. Cf. H. Höffding, *Philosophie de la religion*, French translation, 1909, p. 140ff. [also *The Philosophy of Religion*, transl. B. E. Meyer, London, 1906. R. P.]
47. There is a good example of an analysis of an important formula in O. Dibelius, *Das Vaterunser: Umrisse zu einer Geschichte des Gebets in der alten und mittleren Kirche*, Giessen, 1903. The comparative analysis of dogmas and formulae of belief, of their meaning in the primitive Christian tradition and the meaning they had for Luther, shows strikingly how the meaning and significance of prayer have changed.
48. This applies to individual prayer in the synagogue, *Talm. Babl. Berakhot*, 16a; E. Schürer, op. cit., pp. 25, 45ff.; cf. J.J. Kohler's article 'Prayer', *Jewish Encyclopaedia*, New York, 1901–6, 12 vols.
49. What R. Bekaï said about the Shemoné Esré, the eighteen benedictions, is exactly the opposite of what happened in the synagogue. But his statement contains a just appreciation of the value of canonical formulae: 'And you should know that from the time of Moses, our master, until the days of the great synagogue, the prayer of Israel did not have an established order for all of us, and each among the faithful individually made up his own formula (the sense of the Hebrew word is actually 'enigma')and prayed at will, according to his knowledge and ability and his gift for words; it was then that the men of the great synagogue came along and instituted this prayer, the *Shemoné Esré*, in such a way that there was a prescribed prayer for all Israel.' *Or hahaiim*, p. 113.

    On the history of the *Shemoné Esré*, see I. Loeb, 'Les dix-huit Bénédictions', *Revue des études juives*, 1889, p. 17ff. I. Lévi, 'Des dix-huit Bénédictions et les psaumes de Salomon', *Revue des études juives*, 1896; 'Encore un mot' etc., ibid., p. 161 etc.
50. Cf. Matthew VI, pp. 5–6, on the opposition between individual prayer and the common prayer of the synagogue. But this opposition comes from the synagogue itself and is not a Christian invention.
51. Manu IX, 19 [clearly 18], total prohibition for women; X, 74–80; cf. 'Visnu', II, 1–7. Vasistha, II, 13–19; cf. the texts collected by M. Weber in

Indische Studien, X, 4, p. 17ff.; cf. H. Oldenberg, *Religion du Véda*, transl. V. Henry, Paris, 1903, 316ff.

52. Cf. Strauss, *Brhaspati*, dissertation, and the texts quoted there.
53. Cf. H. Hubert and M. Mauss, 'Essai sur le sacrifice', *Mélanges d'histoire des religions*; Paris, 1907. [Originally 'Essai sur la nature et la fonction du sacrfice', *L'Année sociologique*, I, 1898, pp. 29–138. R. P.]. Cf. P. Oltramare, Le yajamâna, *Muséon*, 1900. We stress 'seem', because in our opinion the texts containing the Vedic ritual have more of a theoretical value than a real historical truth. They do not represent the whole Hindu religion before Buddhism, but only that part which was practised by the various Brahmanical schools.
54. We say 'Hebrew', although very few of the biblical prayer texts (the Song of Deborah is not truly archaic, but merely archaic in form) are pre-exilic. See Cheyne, op. cit., but if this applies to post-exilic religion, we assume that it applies all the more probably to the cult of the first temple before its destruction.
55. Among these is that type of song or popular magico-religious chant, which is, in our view, the most ancient and most primitive fragment of prayer that the Bible has preserved for us, a real chorus of rainmakers: (Numbers XXI, vv. 17–18.) At Béer (the well), Moses brought forth water and Israel sang this song: Spring up, O well! (the first hemistich, which is lacking in the LXX [Septuagint] but is interesting precisely because it gives a magical character to this whole canticle). Sing to it (the well)/ The well that they dug/ the princes dug it/ the nobles of the people/ with their staves of command, with their staves./ (The LXX has another version of the last line. Budde proposes adding to this sort of round the two words *ummidbar mattanâ*, but this is to no purpose, and from this point onwards the text is too corrupt to be emended.) We are grateful to our student, M. Philippe de Félice, who brought the text to our attention.
56. See the other authors quoted above.
57. See J. J. Kohler, *The Psalms and their Place in the Liturgy* (Gratz College Publications), p. 31ff.; cf. *Babylonian Talmud*, Berakhoth tract, 14a, for the way in which the congregation repeated the first line.
58. This is the case in the dedication to the chief cantor, of 55 Psalms etc.
59. We refer especially to the acrostic Psalms, 34, 37 etc.
60. The Song of Songs.
61. I Kings, VIII, vv. 23ff. From v. 29 onwards, it is a question of the people alone.
62. Schürer, op. cit., p. 447ff., notwithstanding the texts quoted by T. K. Cheyne in his article 'Prayer' in *Encyclopaedia Biblica*, London, 1899–1903, p. 3827.
63. Cf. the Roman principle quoted above.
64. See below.

65. The relationships were particularly close in the case of very ancient Roman law, see P. Huvelin, 'Nexum', in C. V. Daremberg and E. Saglio, *Dictionnaire des antiquités*, Paris, 1873–1919.
66. See the examples in E. G. L. Ziebarth, 'Der Fluch im griechischen Rechte', *Hermes*, XXX, 1895.
67. On formalism in general and in Roman law in particular, III, see Iehring, *Esprit du droit*, pp. 156, 255 etc.
68. This is the type of eternity and at the same time of causality, says Manu, II, 84: 'all other activities prescribed by the Vedas are perishable (in themselves and by their feasts, says the commentary), the libations and sacrifices, etc; the *brahman* (or formula), on the other hand, is imperishable and unalterable, and this is Prajâpati (the god who is the ground of all being and the master of all); cf. *Viṣṇu*, 56, 18ff., *Vasiṣṭha*, XXVI, 9, 10.
69. See especially P. Huvelin, 'Magie et droit individuel', *L'Année sociologique*, Vol. X, 1907, pp. 1–47, especially p. 31ff.; E.A. Westermarck, *The Origin and Development of Moral Ideas*, I, London, 1906, p. 568.
70. See the verse in the *Rig Veda*, II, pp. 32, 13; cf. Manu IV, 233.
71. In the Australian societies we shall be studying, the invention of formulae is precisely the privilege of those magicians and bards whom we have shown as acting only because they enjoy social authority and have themselves been influenced by society. 'The Origin of Magic Powers', Hubert and Mauss, *Mélanges*, p. 131ff.
72. What follows will be recognizable as an application of the principles laid down by E. Durkheim, *Règles de la méthode sociologique*, 3rd. edn., Paris, 1907; cf. M. Mauss and P. Fauconnet, 'Sociologie', *Grande Encyclopédie*, 30, 165–76.
73. See below, Book II, Chapter II.
74. However, we should strongly suspect this to be the case, but only where rituals are very clearly established and canons laid down.
75. Thus there is no doubt that the epiclesis in the canon of the mass is a prayer, but we doubt whether that in the Hellenistic papyri is one. See Dom Cabrol, *Les Origines liturgiques*, Paris, 1906. 1st lecture, *La Prière antique*, Paris, 1900. p. 1300.
76. We have tried to give a sample of what we understand by this sort of criticism both in subsequent chapters and in another work: 'L'Origine des pouvoirs magiques', *Mélanges*, p. 131ff.
77. This does not apply to the works of N.W. Thomas.
78. On historical criticism, see C. Seignobos and C.-V. Langlois, *Introduction aux études historiques*, Paris, 1898, Part 1. Naturally, we are not in agreement with the opinions expressed by Seignobos in the second part of the work.
79. See below, Book II, Chapter II.

80. In W. Ellis, 1st edn., Vol. II, p. 1501ff.
81. This is the case in most of the philological works on the Gâthas of the Avesta or the different parts of the various Vedas. See M. Bloomfield, 'On the Relative Chronology of the Vedic Hymns', *Journal of the American Oriental Society*, 1900, XXI. The test of language is one of the best, but it is not the most reliable. In fact, rituals tend to abuse archaic language, even in Australia (cf. below, Book II, Chapter III), and the artificial language of a recent rite may contain more archaic forms than an ancient rite.
82. Cf. C. Bouglé, *Qu'est-ce que la sociologie: La sociologie inconsciente*, Paris, Alcan, 1907.
83. F. M. Müller, *Sanskrit Literature*, London, 1859, p. 49; A. Macdonnel, *A History of Sanskrit Literature*, London, 1900, p. 127.
84. A. F. Loisy has recently applied principles of this sort to the exegesis of the Gospels, which were, above all, according to him, the property of the various Churches; see *Les Evangiles synoptiques*, 'Introduction'. [Possibly *L'Evangile et l'église*, Bellevue, 1903. R. P.]
85. Kohler, op. cit.: cf. above; cf. *Encyclopaedia Biblica*, under 'Hallel'.
86. Hubert and Mauss, 'Essai sur la nature et la fonction du sacrifice', *Mélanges*, 1909.
87. Cf. the references quoted above; to understand this question, see Winternitz, op. cit., pp. 110 and 130 [note 25].
88. Cf. M. Mauss, 'L'Enseignement de l'histoire des religions des peuples non-civilisés à l'Ecole des Hautes Etudes: Leçon d'ouverture', *Revue de l'histoire des religions*, XLV, 1902, pp. 36–55.
89. See below, Book II, Chapter I.
90. See below, Book II, Chapter III, paragraph 5 for an application of this principle.
91. See below.
92. Magical powers (in particular the *mantra*) in Hindu, Buddhist and Brahman mysticism have the same property as has the ascetic, the *yogi*; cf. Patañjali, *Yogasûtra*, Bombay, 1890, IV, I; R. C. Childers, *A Dictionary of the Pali Language*, London, 1875, under *iddhi*, *jhânam*.
93. See H. Hubert and M. Mauss, 'Esquisse d'une théorie générale de la magie', *L'Année sociologique*, VII, p. 14ff.
94. Not having studied the question, we do not know to what extent individual practice discountenanceso the rule of the sect or order, nor if it is possible to have asceticism without a rule of some kind. However, this is not very likely: cf. O. Zöckler, *Askese und Mönchtum*, Frankfurt, 1897, I, p. 170ff.
95. Paul, I. Cor. 14, especially, v. 26; cf. A. Hilgenfeld, 'Die Glossolalie Christengemeinden', *Jahrbuch der Deutschen Theologie*, 1874, p. 589.
96. Manu, II, 120ff [119ff?]. Cf. Tylor, 'Salutations', *Encyclopaedia Britannica*; H. Ling Roth, 'On Salutations', *Journal of the Anthropological Institute*, XIX, 1890, pp. 164–81, especially p. 166ff.

97. Stewart Culin 'The Games of the North American Indians', *24th Annual Report of the Bureau of American Ethnology*, 1907. It shows that the games of the North American Indians are all ancient rites.
98. Thus with reference to the sacrifice of soma in Vedic India, the Rig-Veda says that it is better than the work of ploughing seven times over; see Bergaigne, *La Religion védique*, III, pp. 8–9n.1.
99. A classic example of an erroneous practice is that of the people of Tahiti planting the nails that Cook had given them; they thought they were seeds and that all they had to do was to plant them in order to obtain more.
100. See Hubert and Mauss, *Mélanges*.
101. See below, Book III, Part II, Chapter III.
102. Cf. Hubert and Mauss, 'Esquisse d'une théorie générale de la magie', *L'Année sociologique*, VII.
103. J. G. Frazer, *Golden Bough*, I, p. 20ff. [1st edn., London 1890, 2nd edn. 1900. R. P.].
104. Cf. Hubert and Mauss, 'Esquisse d'une théorie générale de la magie', p. 16ff. Religion, of course, is usually theurgic and magic usually propitiatory, but in differing degrees.
105. Cf. below, Book II, Chapter III.
106. Cf. Hubert and Mauss, 'Origine des pouvoirs magiques', in *Mélanges*.
107. There are numerous examples of the soma sacrifice: M. Caland and V. Henry, *Agnistoma*, I, pp. 13, 14, 26, 27 etc., and on nearly every page. We do not believe, however, that all these rites cease to be religious because they are magic by nature. In the context of ritual, religion vies with magic in using certain actions, things and ideas that are common to both. That is why we disagree with W. Caland (who follows Sten Konow, *Das Sâmaviddhânabrahmana, ein altindisches Handbuch der Zauberei*, 1893), who classes special sacrifices with specific intentions among magic rites (mantras and manual rites) (Caland, 'Over de Wenschoffers', Amsterdam, *Verslagen en Mededelingen der Koninklijk Akademie der Wetenschapen, Afdeling Letterkunde*, IV, V, 1902, p. 436; 'Altindische Zauberei, Darstellungen der Altindischen Wunschopfer', ibid., X, no.1, 1908). We would say that these sympathetic rites and others are part of religion.
108. J.G. Frazer, cf. below; cf. Hubert and Mauss, *Mélanges*, p. xxx.
109. Cf. *Encyclopédie des sciences religieuses* (Lichtenberger), article on 'Prayer'.
110. Thus there is no Church or Christian sect which has not attached the notion of prayer to that of edification (οἰχοδομή), which implies precisely this idea of an act: I. Peter, 2, v. 5; I Cor. 14, v. 4ff.
111. L. Blau, *Altjüdisches Zauberwesen*, Strasbourg, 1901, p. 16ff.
112. The powers of the *mantra* are one of the richest sources of epic and Vedic literature.
113. *Kauśikasûtra* 25, 37, etc. *Atharva-Veda*, I.10, cf. V. Henry, *La magie dans l'Inde*, p. 209.

114. We are referring to the hymn, *Rig-Veda* I.164 = A.V. 9.9–10, used in the *mahâvrata* (*Śaṅkhâyana śrauta sûtra* 16, 22, 7. Cf. Sâyana on R.V. I. 164) and in a rite of prosperity (*Kauśikasûtra* 18, 25), which is also part of the collection of the Upanishads, *Aitareya Aranyaka*, 5.3.2.
115. We believe that these two translations can be reconciled. Those who hold to the second are M. Haug, 'Vedische Rätselfragen und Rätselsprüche', *Sitzungsberichte der phil. mat. Classe d. K. Bayer, Akademie der Wissenschaften*, II; V. Henry, *Atharva Veda*, Books VIII and IX, pp. 107ff., 143ff. Deussen has given the most mystical interpretation in *Allgemeine Geschichte der Philososphie*, I, i, p. 105ff. A bibliography on the subject and a very competent translation may be found in C. R. Lanmann-Whitney, *Atharvaveda Samhita* II, p. 533. (We sincerely thank Harvard University for donating us these superb publications. This and M. Bloomfield's *Vedic Concordance*, Cambridge, Mass., 1906, have been and still are of great value to us, indeed they are indispensable.
116. Blau, loc. cit.; see *Jewish Encyclopaedia*, XXI, p. 713.
117. An excellent account of this historical trajectory of the Atharva-Veda may be found in Bloomfield, *The Atharva Veda*, p. Bff.
118. Cf. Paul, Ephesians, VI, vv. 17, 18: ' And take ... the sword of the spirit which is the word of God. Pray at all times in the Spirit with all prayer and supplication'. [Mauss writes incorrectly Chapter V. R. P.]
119. On the oath in classical antiquity, see E. von der Glotz, article 'Jusjurandum', Daremberg and Saglio, *Dictionnaire des antiquités*; R. Hirzel, *Der Eid*, Leipzig 1902; L. Wenger, 'Der Eid in den griechischen Papyrusurkunden', *Zeitschrift der Savigny Stiftung*, 1902, XXIII, *R. Abth.* pp. 158–274; cf. P. Huvelin, 'Magie et droit individuel', *L'Année sociologique*, X, p. 32n.1, 12; Westermarck, *Origin and Evolution of Moral Ideas*, I, pp. 58–61 etc.
120. See W. H. D. Rouse, *Greek Votive Offerings: An Essay on the History of Greek Religion*, Cambridge 1902.
121. See Rouse, ibid; Andree, *Ueber Votiv- und Weihegaben*.
122. Notice the use of the middle voice in *εὔχομαι, praecor*.
123. Cf. T. K. Cheyne, 'Blessings and Cursings', *Encyclopaedia Biblica*.
124. From this point of view, it is useless to distinguish between the charm and the prayer, as do R.R. Marett and L. Farnell (see below). Not only is there an element of charm in every prayer, even when one adopts their terminology, but it is also inaccurate to exclude all theurgy from all religion.
125. A. Sabatier, *Esquisse*, pp. 23 and 40.
126. *Elements of the Science of Religion*, Edinburgh, 1898, II, p. 150.
127. Ibid., p. 154.
128. Like their imitators, R. Pfleiderer (*Grundriss der Religionsphilosophie*, p. 190); J. F. W. Bousset (*Das Wesen der Religion*, lectures from Göttingen,

Göttingen, 1904, p. 21). A fine anthropologist, A. E. Crawley, fell into the same error. It is true that his work has a philosophical character (*The Tree of Life*, London, 1905, pp. 62 and 182). However, he is familiar with the Australian data and argues against Frazer's interpretation of them, though conducting his debate like a theologian (A. Lang, *Myths, ritual and religions*, London, 1887, Fr. transl., p. 180, has the same attitude).

129. E. Tylor, *Primitive Culture*, London, 1871, II, p. 148.
130. See T. Waitz, *Anthropologie der Naturvölker* (2), Leipzig, 1859–72, IV, p. 508.
131. M. Miller, 'On Ancient Prayer', in *Semitic Studies* (Kohut), Berlin, Calvary, 1896, pp. 1–51. (Extract from a course of unpublished lectures given in Oxford in 1895); cf. Preface to Wyatt Gill, *Myths and Songs of the South Pacific*, London, 1890.
132. R.H. Codrington, *The Melanesians*, Oxford, 1890.
133. Müller, 'Ancient Prayer', p. 41; cf. his *Anthropological Religion*, London, 1893, p. 320.
134. Codrington, op. cit. [n.133], pp. 71, 123.
135. He does not quote it, but the book was successful enough for us to assume that it was known to one of the founders of the science of religions.
136. J. A. Farrer, 'The Prayers of Savages', in *Primitive Manners and Customs*, London, 1872.
137. R. R. Marett, 'From Spell to Prayer', *Folk-Lore*, XV, 1904, pp. 132–65.
138. W. H. R. Rivers, 'On Toda Prayers', *Folk-Lore*, XV, 1904, pp. 166–81.
139. Cf. W. H. R. Rivers, *The Todas*, London, Macmillan, 1906, p. 216ff.; cf. below, L. R. Farnell, *The Evolution of Religion* (Crown Theological Series), London, 1905, Chapter III. 'History of Prayer'.
140. Farnell, op. cit., p. 167; the evidence quoted is taken from an article by M. Latham [actually S. L. Cummins. R. P.], 'The Tribes and Subtribes of the Bahr el Gazal', *Journal of the Anthropological Institute*, 1904, XXXIV, pp. 149–66, especially p. 165. It is not valid. The text simply means that there are no prayers addressed to the great God. Besides, the assertion itself is somewhat improbable because the Nilotic peoples, who have achieved a high degree of civilization, are among the most religious of African peoples.
141. Frazer applied this theory to the magic and religion that would have followed a magical age of humanity; cf. *Golden Bough*, II, p. 140ff.; III, p. 530f.
142. See Hubert and Mauss, 'Esquisse d'une théorie générale de la magie', *L'Année sociologique*, 7, p. 101f.
143. We shall not take the Tasmanian data into account except to make certain references and comparisons, although the natives of Tasmania certainly came from the same stock as the Australians in very primitive times, as is generally accepted; see A.W. Howitt, 'President's Address', *Australasian*

Association for the Advancement of Science, 1898, IV, Melbourne [actually 1907, XI, Adelaide. R.P.]; *Native Tribes of South-East Australia* (henceforward *S. E. A.*), London 1904, Chapter I. All the useful documents may be found in H. Ling Roth's monograph *The Aborigines of Tasmania*, 2nd edn., Halifax, King, 1899. The observation of the Tasmanians, if it could have been undertaken, would have been of first importance to us because they represented a living example of a vanished period of humanity in regions where we have the most ancient paleolithic civilizations; cf. E. B. Tylor, 'On the Tasmanians as Representatives of Palaeolithic Man', *Journal of the Anthropological Institute* (henceforward *J. A. I.*), 1894, XXIII, pp. 141–52. But the Tasmanians were wiped out before any precise observation had been made of the societies they formed. However, the few documents concerning them in no way contradict the data furnished by Australian religions, and some might even be valuable as comparison.

144. O. Schœtensack, 'Die Bedeutung Australiens für die Heranbildung des Menschen aus einer niederen Form', *Zeitschrift für Ethnologie*, 1901, XXXIII, pp. 127–54; cf. H. Klaatsch. *Verhandlungen des Deutschen Anthropologischen Tages zu Frankfurt*, in *Mittheilungen. der Anthropologischen Gesellschaft in Wien*, 1907, p. 83.
145. Not to be confused with the Onans, on which see Bunsen, 'The Onans of Tierra del Fuego', in *Geographical Journal*, 1905, I, p. 513 [not found. R. P.], who are Patagonian immigrants and consequently part of the great race and civilization of the Caribbean. On this, cf. R. Verneau, *Les Patagoniens*, Paris, 1899.
146. P. D. J. Hyades and J. Deniker, *Scientific Mission to Tierra del Fuego*, Vol. IV [also *Mission scientifique du Cap Horn*, Paris, 1891. R. P.]. The observations on religion in particular are hasty and were made under unfavourable conditions.
147. W. J. Mac Gee, 'The Seri Indians', in XVIIth *Annual Report of the Bureau of American Ethnology*, Part 1, Washington, 1898.
148. The lack of 'knowledge of the knife'; Mac Gee, loc. cit. p. 152*, p. 154*; reduction of the social groups to two totemic clans, ill-defined beliefs, p. 269. [meaning of * here and elsewhere is unclear. R. P.]
149. Pottery, soapstone (*olle*) in particular; see Mac Gee, loc. cit. p. 220*, composite arch, p. 195f*.
150. On this point, cf. Mac Gee, loc. cit. p. 293ff*.; Alzadar, *Estudios sobre los Indios del Mexico Norte*, Mexico City, 1903, p. 180f. (which seems to be inspired by Mac Gee's documents).
151. See the bibliography on them, W. Schmidt, 'Die Pygmäer des Ituri', in *Zeitschrift für Ethnologie*, 1905, p. 100ff. [this article is not any volume of *ZfE* for the period up to the 1970s and has not been located, though Schmidt certainly used data from the Ituri in writing elsewhere about the Pygmies. R. P.]; also Mgr Le Roy, *Les Pygmées africains*, Paris, Mame [?], 1905.

152. See the works quoted by W.W. Skeat and C.O. Blagden, *The Pagan Races of the Malay Peninsula*, London, Macmillan, 1906, p. XXXf. On the Negritoes of the Philippines, see the publications of the *Ethnological Survey*, directed by A. E. Jenks; cf. *L'Année sociologique*, X, p. 213 [probably actually p. 251–4, Mauss's review of Jenks, *The Bontoc Igorot*. R. P.]. The latter have almost completely lost their distinctive character.
153. Since it is F. and P. Sarrasin who spread these fables (*Die Veddahs von Ceylon*, Basle, 1888), we await their observations on the Toalas of the Celebes with impatience and some misgivings.
154. On the notion of the geographical province, see A. Bastian, *Das elementare Völkergedanke*, Berlin, 1874 [It is not clear which work by Bastian Mauss has in mind here; there are several with similar titles, but none which precisely matches this one. R. P.]. Let us agree that it is incontestable that Malayan influences were at work in the north of Australia and Oceanic influences in the north-east: see Major Campbell, 'Memorial of Residence at Melville Island and Port Essington', *Journal of the Royal Geographical Society*, 1843, Vol. XIII, p. 180f. [not found. R. P.]; G. Earl, 'On the Aboriginal Tribes of the Northern Coast of Australia', ibid., 1845, Vol. XVI, p. 239; cf. N. Thomas, 'Australian Canoes and Rafts', *J.A.I.*, 1905, type 3, pp. 56–79, especially p. 70. However, the present work could be considered as contributing to establishing the unity of these Australian populations. The only person to have contested this is J. Matthew (*Eaglehawk and Crow*, London, Nutt, 1899), who even sees in the division of the primary clans proof of the existence of two separate races and attributes one to the Papuan branch and the other to the Dravidian branch of humanity. We shall not discuss this thesis, which is not even supported by the linguistic proofs that the author claims to have found. The only points we can grant him are that it is very possible that the Tasmanians are not entirely of the same race and civilization as the Australians but represent an earlier stratum of the population. This conclusion is based on geological (cf. Howitt, loc. cit. [n. 144]) and zoological grounds (the absence of the dingo; cf. *Transactions of the Royal Society of South Australia*, Memoir II), and also for technological reasons (see Tylor, loc. cit. [n. 130]).
155. On this point we simply refer the reader to the works of the ethnographers. We have considerable reservations about many of them, but they are nonetheless valuable. See G. Waitz, *Anthropologie der Naturvölker*, IV, 2; Robert Brough Smyth, *Aborigines of Victoria*, 2 vols, Melbourne 1878, I, p. lxxxff.; E.M. Curr, *The Australian Race*, Melbourne, 1886 (4 vols.), I, p. 28ff.; Howitt, loc. cit. [n. 144]; Schœtensack, op. cit. [n. 145]; F. Graebner, 'Kulturstadien und Kulturkreise in Australien und Melanesien' [presumably 'Kulterkreise und Kulturschichten in Ozeanian'. R. P.], *Zeitschrift für Ethnologie*, 1905, XXXVII, p. 410ff.

[actually pp. 28–53. R. P.]. The first observers had already noted these uniformities, especially of a linguistic sort; see J. Eyre, *Journey of Discovery*, etc., 1835, II, appendix [cf. n. 166 for full reference under this name, though with different initials and date of publication. R. P.]

156. See P. Topinard, *Les Indigènes australiens*, Paris, 1878; Helms, 'Anthropology', in *Transactions of the Royal Society of South Australia*, 1895, Vol. XVII.

157. We regard as established the results of Howitt's studies on types of initiation (cf. *S. E. A.*, conclusion, p. 618ff.), and Thomas's on the nautical arts; cf. op. cit. [n. 155]. We are already obliged to hold as slightly suspect the works of these same authors, however distinguished they may be on matrimonial classes, see Howitt, ibid., p. 150ff.; N. Thomas, *The Marriage Laws of Australians*, Cambridge University Press, 1906. The hypothesis advanced by A. van Gennep on this same subject, of a double origin of the system of filiation, is without foundation (*Mythes et légendes d'Australie*, Paris, Maisonneuve, 1906, p. xc). F. Graebner basically adopts it and without much further argument ('Kulturschichten und Sozialverhältnisse in Australien', *Globus*, 1906, I, pp. 323, 373 etc.). In our opinion, nothing has been proved except the existence of these types and trends. But we expect more from the constitution of a comparative technology and comparative philology of the Australians than from works that immediately raise too many poorly understood sociological questions. However, there is a clear and accurate account in Thomas's work of a certain number of customs concerning family systems.

158. J. G. Frazer, 'The Beginnings of Totemism and Religion', *Fortnightly Review*, 1905; B. Spencer, 'Presidential Address', *Australian Association for the Advancement of Science*, 1904, VIII, p. 160 (primitiveness of the Arunta), contra Howitt, *S. E. A.*, p. 150f. [p. 151ff.]; A. Lang, *The Secret of the Totem*, London, 1905, p. 175; A. van Gennep, *Mythes*, op. cit., p. lxxx; cf. N. W. Thomas in *Man*, 1904, 40; 1905, 42 [both references unclear. R. P.]; 1906, 42 [Mauss's review of Parker, *Euahlayi Tribe*, *L'Année sociologique*, 10, 1907, pp. 230–33, R. P.], which follows after Durkheim, 'Totémisme', *L'Année sociologique*, V, 1902; VIII, 1905 [Mauss has VIII, 1903–1904, R. P.].

159. B. Spencer and F. J. Gillen, *The Native Tribes of Central Australia*, 1899, London, Macmillan, 1899 (henceforward *N. T.*), *The Northern Tribes of Central Australia*, 1904, London, Macmillan, 1904 (henceforward *N. T. C.*), will be among our principal sources. Spencer and Gillen were both fortunate enough to have been considered 'completely initiated' among the Arunta (cf. *N. T. C.*, p. xi) and because of this they had access to many spectacular events, traditions and practices which, even for observers more gifted than they were, would have remained secret. However,

although we make a special case of their works, we shall not follow them blindly. Further on the reader will find much discussion of the documents they have transmitted to us. The spirit in which this discussion will be conducted is as follows: first, it seems certain to us that the Arunta have been much more influenced by European civilization than Spencer and Gillen are willing to show us; cf. *N. T.* p. 12 and Revd Louis Schulze, 'Notes on the Aborigines of the Finke River', *Transactions of the Royal Society of South Australia*, 1891, vol. XIV, II, p. 218. Since the establishment of the station at Alice Springs (to which there has been a regular coach service for several years; cf. R. Mathews, 'Notes on the Languages of Some Tribes of Central Australia', *Journal of the Royal Society of New South Wales*, XXXVIII, p. 420), many practices may have lost their original character. All this concerns the Arunta themselves. As for the observers, we must make a distinction. It is Gillen who seems to have a profound knowledge of Arunta customs, having been a protector of the natives of that region for twenty years; and both authors seem to have only a sketchy knowledge of the other tribes, both of them having acquired this knowledge under more or less similar conditions. However, if this study of the Arunta was extremely profound, it was so only for a few years (cf. the documents which Gillen sent to E. C. Stirling for Section IV, *Anthropology*, of the *Report on the Horn Expedition*, p. 179f.). It was not equally detailed on all points (cf. *L'Année sociologique*, II, pp. 219 and 221 [reference not clear. R. P.]), so we have knowledge of a mere thirteen Intichiuma out of nearly a hundred which must exist, at least if the principles laid down are correct, and without Strehlow we would not know their formulae. Also, the study really refers only to the groups of Alice Springs and the surrounding area. This accounts for the considerable differences we shall notice from the documents of the German missionaries of the Herrmannsburg Mission, on the banks of the Finke. There is a lack of discipline in Spencer and Gillen's study; they seem to have put too much trust in the two intelligent old men with whom they were in touch (cf. *N. T. C.* p. xiii and R. Mathews, loc. cit., p. 420; cf. H. Klaatsch, 'Schlussbericht über meine Reise nach Australien in den Jahren 1904–1907', *Zeitschrift für Ethnologie*, XXXIX, 1907, pp. 635–90). They did not find out if others apart from themselves had already begun the work, and even made considerable progress in it. They could have obtained valuable help, especially from the philological angle, from the missionaries; cf. H. Kempe, 'Grammar and Vocabulary of the Languages Spoken by the Aborigines of the Macdonnell Ranges' (South Australia), *Transactions of the Royal Society of South Australia*, Vol. XIV, I, f.; cf. W. Planert (according to the missionary Wettengel), 'Australische Forschungen, I, Aranda Grammatik', *Zeitschrift für Ethnologie*, XXXIX, 1907, pp. 551–66; and H. Basedow, 'Vergleichende Vokabularen der

Aluridja- und Arunndta-Dialekte Zentralaustraliens', *Zeitschrift für Ethnologie*, XL, 1908, pp. 207–28. Spencer and Gillen are both equally ungifted from a philological point of view and have no system of transcription; for example, whereas Planert, a professional linguist, writes *atua* (man) in phonetic script, they spell it *ertwa*, which gives only an approximation of the sound according to the rules of English pronunciation. They did not make a collection of texts in Arunta, nor an accurate lexicon, and do not know the languages of the neighbouring tribes. We cannot even be sure that they ever communicated with their Arunta brethren except in 'pidgin English', and this would be even more likely to be the case with the other tribes, the Urabunna of the south and the Warramunga of the north in particular. We shall be giving numerous proofs of what we have just stated. In these circumstances, it is all the more regrettable that these authors should not have taken more trouble to give us the names of their informants, the conditions of each of their observations, etc. Nevertheless, we greatly admire the marvellous sense of facts, and especially interesting facts, demonstrated by these two observers. Older and more recent works by the missionaries C. Strehlow, *Die Aranda Stämme*, published by F. v. Leonhardi, Veröffentlichungen von dem Städtlichen Völkermuseum, Frankfurt am Main, 1907, I, *Mythologie der Aranda und Loritja* (the Luritcha of Spencer and Gillen), Kempe (op. cit.) and Schulze (op. cit.) often provide us with sufficient material for critical judgment.

160. W. E. Roth has published: 1) *Ethnological Studies among the North-West-Central Queensland Aborigines*, Brisbane, Government Printer, 1897 (henceforward *Ethn. Res.*); and 2) 8 fascicules of *North Queensland Ethnography Bulletin*, Brisbane, Government Printer, 1900–1907. His observations are drier and more concise but more sporadic and widely scattered than those of Spencer and Gillen; the simplistic explanation (except in technological or strictly ethnographical matters) is a hindrance in many of his observations. We do not know if Roth really told Klaatsch (cf. 'Schlussbericht über meine Reise', p. 739 [p. 639? R. P.]) that he had never come across a totem in Queensland (contra, cf. Roth's texts quoted below on calling animals by their homonyms). In any case, such an idea vitiates his observations: totemism is in fact one of the customs which people like to keep secret, and one must search in order to find it.

161. See Strehlow and Leonhardi, *Die Aranda Stämme* etc. Frankfort, 1907.

162. Howitt, (*S. E. A.*); for earlier works, which Howitt does not even mention completely, see bibliography in *S. E. A.*. Howitt had a personal and profound knowledge only of the Kurnai of Gippsland; his observations were reported by Fison (then resident in the Fiji Islands and who sometimes travelled to Australia) and indirectly by Morgan, to whom

Fison and Howitt made known the terminologies of group kinship and to whom they dedicated their first work (L. Fison and A.W. Howitt, *The Kamilaroi and Kurnai*, London and Melbourne, 1880). But these observations were made twenty years after the European settlement of the country (north-east Victoria); they were for a long time incomplete and, for example, when Howitt realised the existence of initiation, he had to have the ceremonies performed for him; see 'The Jeraeïl or Initiation Ceremonies of the Kurnai Tribe', *J. A. I.*, XIV, 1885, p. 455 [actually 301–25. R. P.] The same applies to the ceremonial combat; *S. E. A.* pp. 344–5. On the other hand, although the observations were carried out with real precision, certain points, mythology for example, were perforce neglected because of the disappearance of the old men who had a knowledge of the traditions; cf. *Kamilaroi and Kurnai* p. 252; 'On Australian Medicine Men', *J. A. I.* XIII, 1884, p. 413 [article not found. R. P.]. In fact, they were only taken down with relative philological precision, as Howitt used mainly the English of the natives (cf. *S. E. A.*, p. 627) and had the phrases or words that interested him dictated to him and sometimes translated with some measure of care and a certain linguistic sense; see the example in *S. E. A.*, p. 630; cf. regarding the Kuringal and Yuin, pp. 533–4. The other tribe, which Howitt knows less well, is the Dieri. He was one of the first Europeans to explore them (cf. 'Personal Reminiscences of Central Australia', *Inaugural Address to the Australasian Association for the Advancement of Science*, Adelaide, 1907, pp. 31ff. (Dieri, Yantruwanta, Yaurorka). He visited them often, but it was only to complete or verify Gason's earlier observations or the recent ones of the missionary, Siebert. Howitt had more or less direct access to other tribes of south-east Australia. Those whom he grouped under the name of Yuin (in the mountains of north-east Victoria and the south-east coast of New South Wales), he observed only after they had been well and truly adulterated by European civilization (for them too he also had to request a performance of their initiation ceremonies; cf. 'On Some Australian Ceremonies of Initiation', *J. A. I.* , XIII, 1884, 410 [actually 432–59. R. P.]). Further, he had only moderately intimate relations with them through the mediation of natives of varying degrees of qualification, who were not all questioned with equal thoroughness (thus Howitt did not learn all he could have about initiation ceremonies from Berak, an old native who was later interrogated by Mathews, cf. below.). For all the other tribes, except those around Maryborough, Howitt used information supplied by colonials who had more or less close relations with the neighbouring tribes.

163. J. D. Woods, *The Native Tribes of South Australia*, Adelaide, 1875.
164. G. de Grey, *Journal of Two Expeditions of Discovery into the Interior of Western Australia*, 2 vols., London, 1835.

165. L. d'Eyre, *Journals of Expeditions of Discovery into Australia* etc., including *An Account of the Manners and Customs of the Aborigines,* 2 vols., London, 1845 (the tribe of Adelaide after Moorhouse, the tribes of the lower Murray after personal observations made over about three years and after serious efforts).
166. The principle works deserving mention are those of C. G. Teichelmann and C.W. Schürmann, *Vocabulary of the Tribes Neighbouring Port Lincoln,* 1834; L. Threlkeld, *A Key to the Structure of the Aboriginal Language Spoken by the Awabakal Tribe of Port Macquarie,* Sydney, 1850 etc.; *An Awabakal English Lexicon,* ibid., reprinted with other works by this author and other authors (A. Günther, Wiraïjuri, etc; Livingstone, Tribes of the Wimmera) in J. Fraser, L. Threlkeld, *A Grammar,* etc. Sydney, 1892; the reprint is neither complete nor perfect; W. Ridley, *Kamilaroi, Dippil and Turrubul: Languages spoken by Australian Aborigines,* 2nd edn., Sydney, 1875, New South Wales Government Printer; Revd Hey, in W. E. Roth, *North Queensland Ethnography Bulletin, 6,* 'A Grammar of the Nggerikudi Language'; Revd Gale, 9, *Bulletin,* 7, 'A Grammar of the Kokowarra and Kokoyimidir Languages' etc. Finally, among the recent documents of German missionaries, we have an important group of texts from the Arunta and Loritja, translated word for word (see above for grammars and lexicons). We shall use only with a certain amount of caution Mathews' rather disorderly linguistic works and the vocabularies published by Brough Smyth (*The Aborigines of Victoria,* Melbourne, 1878, II, pp. 1ff, 310) and E.M. Curr.
167. See A. Crawley, *The Tree of Life,* London, 1906, p. 80. Pater W. Schmidt seems obliged to come to the same conclusion in his articles on 'L'Origine de l'idée de dieu' (*Anthropos,* 1908, III, pp. 125–62, 336–68, 559–611, 801–36, 1081–1120), since he accepts as certain the documents of Mrs Langloh Parker, which we discuss later. Cf. A. Lang, 'Preface' to Parker, *The Euahlayi Tribe; Magic and Religion,* London, 1901, p. 36ff.
168. J. G. Frazer, 'The Origin of Totemism', in *The Fortnightly Review,* 1899. 'Remarks on Totemism'. *J. A. I.* , 1899, p. 280; *Golden Bough,* 2nd edn., London, 1904, p. 363n.1 (see the passages quoted in *L'Année sociologique,* V, p. 212 [review of Frazer by Mauss, R. P.]); 'On Some Ceremonies of the Central Australian Tribes', in *Australasian Association for the Advancement of Science,* Melbourne, VIII, 1901, pp. 312–22. Frazer has recently modified these statements and sees the outlines of what he calls prayer, that is, propitiatory prayer, and of sacrifice in Australian religions; see 'The Beginnings of Religion and Totemism among the Australian Aborgines', in *Fortnightly Review,* 1905, II, pp. 162–72, especially p. 168. However, B. Spencer, 'Totemism in Australia', *Presidential Address to the Australasian Association for the Advancement of Science,* Dunedin Meeting, 1904, pp. 376ff., and F.J. Gillen, 'Magic amongst the Natives of Australia', *Australasian Association for the Advancement of Science,* 1901, Melbourne,

VIII, pp. 162ff. [actually pp. 109ff. R.P.], adhere to their former views. For the record, we make mention of the dubious opinions of P. Topinard, *Les Sauvages australiens,* Paris, 1887, p. 21, and the negative opinions of E. Reclus, *Les Primitifs*, 2nd edn., Paris, 1903, p. 231.

169. For example, those of the negro Andy, an impostor, on all the tribes of New South Wales, in Manning, 'The Aborigines of New South Wales', *Journal of the Royal Society of New South Wales*, 1892, pp. 160–161. [not located. R.P.]
170. Among others, Manning (the Kamilaroi of the East), (Thuruwul), Port-Macquarie, loc. cit., p. 161, which contradicts Threlkeld, loc. cit.[n. 178], below; Wyndham (the Kamilaroi of the West), 'The Aborigines of Australia', *Journal and Proceedings of the Royal Society of New South Wales,* 1889, XXIII, pp. 36–7 (prayers to Baiame), but the document seems to us to come from Andy (cf. Andy, in J. G. Frazer, 'The Aborigines of N. S. W.', *Journal and Proceedings of the Royal Society of New South Wales*, 1889, XVIII, p. 166. Wrixen (the tribe of Melbourne), in a discussion of a communication in the *Proceedings of the Royal Colonial Institute,* London, 1890. XXII, p. 47. The best testimony of this kind is James Dawson's, *The Present State of Australian Aborigines in North West Victoria,* Melbourne, 1822, p. 210 [impossible to locate this. 1822? R. P.]
171. J. Oxley, *Journals of Two Expeditions into the interior of New South Wales*, etc. London, 1820, p. 162.
172. Tribe of the River Barcoo (probably the Barkunji group), in Curr, *Australian Race*, II, no. 107, p. 377.
173. W. A. Pechey, 'Vocabulary of the Cornu Tribe' (the Wiraijuri group), *J.A.I.*, 1872, p. 143; see under *coola-boor*, 'god'.
174. Yualeai in certain other authors, New South Wales, River Barwan (organization and language of the Kamilaroi type).
175. L. Parker, *Australian Legendary Tales,* London, 1897, p. x; *More Australian Legendary Tales,* London, 1899, p. 96. We are not sure if Mrs. Parker attended this ceremony herself, since she says herself in her last book, *The Euahlayi Tribe*, p. 89, that she had been told that this rite would have been performed 'in other circumstances'.
176. *Bullimah* also means crystal; the magic crystal, which forms the shoulders of Baiaime, is at the same time the celestial substance and supremely beautiful; cf. *Australian Legendary Tales*, p. 91.
177. Wundah, the evil spirit in these languages. Cf. Günther's vocabulary (Wiraijuri) in L. Threlkeld (Fraser ed.), *ad verbum*. We do not understand Eleanbah; but one can see how close we are to the notion of hell; cf. *The Euahlayi Tribe*, p. 78; Eleanbah Wundah, 'great fire, perpetual motion'.
178. *The Euahlayi Tribe*, p. 8.
179. Cf. C. Richards, 'crying heart', in Wiraijuri vocabulary, 'The Wiraa-dthooree, etc. Science of Man', *Australasian Anthropological Journal*

(henceforward *Science of Man*), 1903, VI, p. 320; cf. F. Tuckfield in J. J. Cary, *Vocabulary of the Geelong and Colac Tribes*, 1840; *Australian Association for the Advancement of Science*, 1898, Sydney, VII, pp. 863–4; all this surely comes from the Anglican *Book of Common Prayer*.

180. Cf. *The Euahlayi Tribe*, p. 76, the existence of many half-breeds, the severe attitude of the old *wirreenun* towards the lapse of traditional customs.
181. Preface to *Australian Legendary Tales*, p.iii.
182. We do not in the least deny that, under European influence, this custom could easily have taken root; certain ideas, peculiar to these tribes, made it possible, in particular, the relationship which exists between the rank of initiation and the state of the soul after death (see below, Book II, Chapter V).
183. See S. Reinach, 'L'Origine des prières pour les morts', in *Cultes, mythes et religions*, Paris, Leroux, 1905, p. 316. Perhaps in Egyptian or Anatolian Christianity, these rites proceed from mystical sources, but it is impossible to say if the latter are themselves ancient or recent.
184. *The Euahlayi Tribe*, p. 85, unless the *Goohnai* of the burial of old Eerin (*More Australian Legendary Tales*) is the same as this one, and unless in all this there are serious errors in transcription.
185. *The Euahlayi Tribe*, p. 89.
186. Pronounced like English: *Bura*, ordinarily written *bora*. Mrs Parker speaks of the initiation ceremonies only by hearsay and, what is more, in the past tense: the rites had fallen into disuse by the time she finally gathered or was able to gather her material together.
187. *The Euahlayi Tribe*, pp. 79–80. See the discussion of this same text by R.R. Marett, 'Australian Prayer', *Man*, 1907, pp. 2–3, and A. Lang, whose reply is in ibid., pp. 67–9; Marett replies in ibid., pp. 114–5.
188. *The Euahlayi Tribe*, p. 79.
189. *The Euahlayi Tribe*, p. 80, on which see below, Book II, Chapter V.
190. *The Euahlayi Tribe*, p. 79.
191. Here again we do not deny that there were elements in the Australian religions that made this borrowing possible. Certain examples will be found below, because it is known that the gods, in certain cases, are said to require the observance of the *bora* (see Book II, Chapter VI, on the religious character.)
192. Some of these facts are in A.W. Howitt, *S. E. A.* , pp. 523, 528, 543; cf. below, Book II, Chapter V.
193. We refer to the rites which we group below under the name of *yibai-malian*, Book II, Chapter V, i, which is connected with the totemic cult of initiation, the giving of the name and the cult of the great gods of the initiation.
194. *More Australian Legendary Tales*, p. 94ff.
195. *The Euahlayi Tribe*, p. 80. On p. 79 we find evidence that Mrs Parker must have spoken about prayer to her native informers, because they reply, as the American Indian did to Oglethorpe, that to them daily prayers seemed

to be an insult to Baiame. They certainly made the responses to him which they believed were demanded of them.

196. *Australian Race*, I, pp. 44–5: 'what is certain is that nothing in the nature of a cult, of prayer or of sacrifice has been observed'.
197. *S. E. A.*, p. 503.
198. *N. T. C.*, p. 491; 'There is never an idea of appealing to any *alcheringa* ancestor'. Strehlow himself, who does however, affirm the existence of the gods, *altjira*, did not find prayer in the Arunta (in the way he understands the word); see N. W. Thomas, 'The Religious Ideas of the Arunta.' *Folk-Lore*, XVI, 1905, pp. 428–33, especially p. 430.
199. See loc. cit. [n. 160]
200. E. Stevens, 'The Aborigines of South Australia', *Journal of the Royal Society of New South Wales*, 1889, Vol. XXIII, p. 482.
201. Herbert and Burnett Rivers (group of the Dora, *Kumbiningerri*, etc.); cf. R. H. Mathews, 'The Toara Ceremony of the Dippil Tribes of Queensland', *American Anthropologist*, II (n.s.), 1, 1900, pp. 139–44, especially 139; 'The Thoorga Language, etc., in Notes on the Language', etc, *Journal of the Royal Geographical Society of Queensland*, XIII, p. 200; see R. W. Semon, *In the Australian Bush*, London, 1891, p. 230 (also denies the existence of any religion).
202. In their evangelization, Mrs J. Smyth says that she and the missionaries found no system of worship to overthrow; B. Smyth, *The Booandik Tribe*, etc., Adelaide, 1880, p. 33.
203. T. Petrie, 'Notes on the Aborigines of Australia', in *Special Volume of the Proceedings of the Geographical Society of Australia*, Sydney, 1865, pp. 76–7.
204. J. Mann, *Mémoires historiques de l'Australie Occidentale*, transl. Falcimane, Paris, 1845, p. 259.
205. p. 345, despite the interpretation given on p. 200 of the corroboree as constituting a mass; cf. Jalaru: dance, p. 345.
206. See the lexicons already mentioned, e.g., C. G. Teichelmann and C.W. Schürmann, in Wilhelmi, *Evangelische Missionszeitschrift*, Basle, 1870, p. 31ff.
207. The Gospel according to St. Luke (new edition by Fraser), *Wiyelli-ela*, p. 129, cf. [Chapter I, R. P.] , vv. 19–20, my word, my words, *wyellikanne*, ibid., Chapter II, v. 34, p. 34; ibid. Chapter III, v. 21; *wyelliela*, making his prayer; ibid., Chapter IV, v. 19, meaning to announce, cf. vv. 7, 10; ibid., Chapter IX, v. 29; *wyelliela*, prayer (of Jesus); ibid., vv. 22, 40, p. 187, *wyella*, to pray; ibid., vv. 41–3, 45, *wyella*, to speak; cf. *A Grammar*, p. 10, on the meaning of the word *wya*, amen: to pray, *ewyelliko*; cf. *A Key to the Awabakal*, p. 112, *s.v. wya*, see *wyellikane*, one who speaks, who calls.
208. In Curr, *Australian Race*, II, p. 92.
209. These are the languages of the upper river Yarra, Brough Smyth, *Aborigines of Victoria*, II, p. 128; cf. p. 132. [n.156]

210. Indeed, in general there are few which have been more clearly classified by the ethnographers among magic rites, but it is pointless to oppose the errors of some of them with those of others; cf. below, Book III, Chapter I, magic rites. For some of these rites, this is completely unjustified; cf., below, Book II, Chapter II. But it is very likely that this classification is the result of an already venerable tradition in anthropology to which questionnaires, especially those of the Geographical Society of London, the Anthropological Institute and even Frazer's, lent their authority.
211. D. Bunce, *Australasiatic Reminiscences*, Melbourne, 1857, p. 73, quoted by Brough Smyth, *Aborigines of Victoria*, I, pp. 127–8. Bunce is an excellent observer and has a good knowledge of the language.
212. The Geelong tribe (Bunurong group) .
213. We can verify the meaning of two words in this translation with the help of Bunce's vocabulary, in B. Smyth, *Aborigines of Victoria*, II, p. 134.
214. On facts of the same kind, see below. We stress the word 'it', which would denote that *marmingatha* is not a divinity but the storm itself.
215. B. Smyth II, p. 141, *marmingatha*, divine, minister, Lord, Supreme Being, orison, a prayer, religion; *marmingatha ngamoodjitch*, preacher (cf. *ngamoordijitch marmingatha*, p. 145, parson, priest). The history of the word seems to have been as follows: *marmingatha* was used at the beginning of the Lord's Prayer which they tried to teach to the Geelong people, and which ended up by meaning everything to do with evangelical religion.
216. *Marmoonth*, father; ibid., p. 141; *marmingatha* must mean 'our father'.
217. Cf. in connection with the tribe of the upper Yarra river (another Bunurong group) a document by Thomas, in B. Smyth, *Aboriginal Victorians*, I, p. 466, a *marminarta*, a spirit which takes possession of an old man.
218. Mrs L. Parker, *The Euahlayi Tribe*, p. 12; cf. an equivalent children's rite in the Dieri tribe, S. Gason, in Curr, *Australian Race*,. II, p. 92. See below, Chapter V, for rites of the same kind.
219. S. Gason, *The Manners and Customs of the Diyerie Tribe of Australian Aborigines*, Melbourne, 1874 [also Adelaide, 1879. R. P.], reprinted in J. D. Woods, *The Native Tribes of South Australia*, 1886, and in Curr (from whom we quote), *The Australian Race.*, II, 55, pp. 66 and 68. Cf. S. Gason to Howitt [actually to J. G. Frazer. R. P.], 'Of the Tribes Dieyerie etc.', *J. A. I.*, XXIV, pp. 167–76, esspecially p. 175 (it is also Moora Moora who inspires the rites).
220. See below, Chapter III, 4.
221. On the general value of rainmaking rites, one of the best assessments is that of old D. Collins, *An Account of the English Colony of New South Wales*, 2nd edn., London, 1801, p. 555. [The date of 1801 seems to be wrong. According to Hubert and Mauss, 'Magie' (cf. Mauss, *Oeuvres*, II, p. 333),

there are two editions of this work, dated 1798 and 1804 respectively. Since the 1804 edition is cited there, we can probably assume that Mauss used it in *Prayer* too. R. P.]

222. J. G. Frazer has recently pointed to a certain number of facts which we set down here and has clearly shown that they constitute the beginnings of prayer, even understood as propitiatory: 'Beginnings of Religion', p. 164.
223. We leave on one side the question of whether they are the totems of individuals or of the clan.
224. River Tully, North Queensland; see W. E. Roth, 'Superstition, Magic, and Medicine', *Bulletin*, 5, 7, pp. 20–1. As Roth does not write very well, our translation is not as literal as those we normally provide.
225. Roth, who does not believe in totemism, means here matrimonial classes.
226. For example, in what Roth, in showing a certain systematising tendency, calls the ceremonial games imitating animals, 'Games, Sports and Amusements.' *Bulletin*, 4, p. 8n.1; p. 28n.4. [p. 28 not found. R. P.]
227. Roth's sentence is dreadful. 'If there is some noise, cry or call which must be made at the same time, one can imitate it'. But at a pinch one can see that it is a question of the cry of an animal that is made in many totemic ceremonies (cf. 'Games etc.', loc. cit. [?]; cf. below, Chapter IV, 3).
228. A remarkable case of hostile totems. In order to understand the text, one must compare it with the one we quote below, which explains it, p. 122n.4 [?]. The fact may seem extraordinary, but it is not so in many Australian societies. Certain totems are of a dangerous nature and their cult consists rather in entreating them to do no harm. On the other hand, it is not foreign to the nature of the totem to be dangerous to its human companion, particularly in the case of a violation of totemic prohibitions (see sanctions, below, Book III, Chapter IV). Even the soul may be dangerous for the individual who possesses it, because it is exterior to him; thus in the the Pennefather tribe (Roth, 'Superstition, Magic, and Medicine', 5, p. 29n.116), the *choi* or the *ngai* living in a tree can cause their man who climbs it to fall.
229. A case of consuming the totem, which has nothing to do with the totemic sacrament as practised by the Arunta. Is it confined to times of famine? The wording 'should he be hungry' might perhaps lead us to believe so.
230. There is a rain clan in this tribe, ibid., p. 9, sect. 16. This clan also seems to have lightning and thunder among its sub-totems.
231. To make thunder? Probably to make it stop.
232. Ibid., p. 37, sect. 150; cf. ibid., p. 26n.104 (seems to be the same thing).
233. Ibid., pp. 20–1, sect. 74.
234. River Proserpine, Koko-yimidir, Roth, ibid., p. 21, sect. 74. On the matrimonial classes, see Durkheim, 'La Prohibition de l'inceste et ses origines', *L'Année sociologique*, I, 1898, p. 11. Long debates between observers and theorists have added nothing to the proposed theory and

have not really contradicted it, so we shall leave it alone. Let us say simply that all Australian societies, except a small number, have this organization. They are divided into four, in certain cases eight classes, which are again divided into two phratries, within which all marriage is forbidden. An individual of a given class may only marry an individual of a given class in another phratry, the children being necessarily in another class from those of the ascendant from which they take their filiation (father or mother according to the case, the object of the system of eight classes being to take into account both lines of descent, in the phratries and in the totems; see Durkheim, 'Sur l'organization matrimoniale des sociétés australiennes' in *L'Année sociologique*, VIII, p. 116ff.) A good exposé of the facts and doctrines, especially comprehensive from the point of view of the documents, is by N. Thomas, *Kinship Organizations and Group Marriage in Australia* (Cambridge Archaeological and Ethnological Series I, Cambridge University Press, 1906). The Proserpine tribe, with the Wakelbura, Pegullobura, the Port Mackay tribe etc., is among those who classify things according to matrimonial classes. Cf. Durkheim and Mauss, 'De quelques formes primitives de classification', *L'Année sociologique*, VI, 1903, p. 12; cf. below, Book III, Chapter III. These are the divisions:

Kurchilla: rainbow, opossum, land guana, spotted lizard
Kupuru: 'stinging tree', emu, eel, tortoise
Banbari: honey, 'sting ray', bandicoot, eagle-falcon
Wungko: wind, rain, brown snake, carpet snake.

235. We say auxiliary animal here because, even if there is a totem, and however rare this kind of totemism may be in Australia, it is evidently thought of as auxiliary. What is more, the difference which exists between Australian totemism and others on this point has been exaggerated, above all by B. Spencer, 'The Totemism in Australia', VIII, *Meeting of the Australasian Association for the Advancement of Science*, 1904, p. 80 [? p. 380?] ; we shall establish this below, Book III, II, Chapter IV.
236. See below, Book II, Chapter IV, last paragraph.
237. On the Pitta Pitta, see Roth, *Ethn. Res.*, pp. 57–58; cf. Roth in *Proceedings of the Royal Society of Queensland*, 1897, 24[?]; 'Food, its Quest and Capture', etc., *Bulletin*, VII, p. 31, sect. 102.
238. Cf. above, p. 121n.2, p. 122n.1, and below, Chapter III.
239. This tribe is certainly attached to the central Australia group; cf. Howitt, *S. E. A.*, p. 111; cf. Spencer and Gillen, *N. T. C.*, p. 70.
240. C. W. Schürmann, 'The Aboriginal Tribe of Port Lincoln', in Woods, *Native Tribes*, p. 219 [n.164]. The word *ngaitye* meant 'totem' in these and the neighbouring tribes (already belonging to another kind of civilization) and meant 'my flesh'; cf. G. Taplin, *Grammar of the Narinyerri Tribe of Australian Aborigines*, Adelaide, 1878, p. 2. In the light of the

document just quoted, therefore, Schürmann has translated incorrectly and should have said, 'my flesh! my flesh, my totem'. Perhaps the rite even had a very complex meaning which we shall never be able to unravel (the word *ni-ngaitye*, the priors (sic.) [pray-ers?], Taplin, ibid., p. 64, may have corresponded to this totemic practice).

241. Schürmann, ibid., p. 220; cf. J. Eyre, *Journeys of Discovery*, II, pp. 333–334 (on the tribe located near Adelaide), seems to have verified these assertions.
242. Cf. C. G. Teichelmann and C. W. Schürmann in Wilhelmi, 'Die Eingeborenen, etc.', in *Aus allen Weltteilen*, I, 1870, p. 13. These texts are analysed below, Book II, Chapter VI, because they give a good idea of the conglomerate of formulae from which all this began. Cf. also Chapter V, paragraph [section?] 5, for a general explanation of these forms of the totemic cult.
243. Intichiuma, see Chapter III, totemic ceremonies, sections 3, 4 and 7.
244. On the totemic cult of the Wollunqua, see Book II, Chapter VI, where we shall show the religious character of all the ritual of the Australian clans, phratries, tribes and nations, and indicate their possible evolution.
245. Klaatsch's sarcastic comments against the very clear statements of Spencer and Gillen prove nothing (see 'Schlussbericht über meine Reise nach Australien in den Jahren 1904–1907', *Zeitschift für Ethnologie*, 1907, p. 636). What is evident is that these rites form part not only of the totemic cult but also of the snake cult, and the cult of water snakes in particular. But this in no way contradicts the observations of the English authors.
246. *N. T. C.*, pp. 252–253; cf. p. 495.
247. Henceforward, we shall use the (Australian) English word 'waterhole' as a translation, which is equivalent to neither the French words *fontaine* [fountain, R.P.], *source* [spring, R.P.], nor to a periphrasis like *puits naturel* [natural well, R.P.]. These are the cavities normally produced in the rocks from which water trickles out and where it collects.
248. This sentence disappears from the account of the ceremony, p. 495.
249. Cf. *N. T. C.*, pp. 227–8, 495–496.
250. On this meaning of the rite, see Frazer, 'Beginnings of Religion' , p. 165.
251. On Karnmari, see Roth, *Ethn. Res.*, pp. 152, 260; vocabulary, p. 198; 'Superstition, Magic, Medicine', *Bull.*, V. p. 29n.118 (cf. below, Book III, Chapter IV, 5, on the spirits of nature).
252. *Ethn. Res.* p. 160n.276; 'Superstition, Magic, Medicine', p. 26n.104. These two documents differ slightly but are fundamentally in agreement.
253. The proof of this meaning of the rite is that they do not dare to cross the river if they have someone with them (Roth, 'Superstition, Magic, Medicine', p. 26).
254. See below, Book III, origin of the ritual formula.

255. On this question of the great god, see below.
256. The fact that this great god is often a totem or an ancient totem, or a kind of archetype of the totems, or a hero who brought civilization, in no way rules out his celestial nature.
257. See *N. T. C.*, pp. 498–9, 344–7. On the neighbouring myth of the two *Tumana* (the sound of the *churinga*: devils), see p. 421; cf. 499–500. The name 'Atnatu' comes from *atna*, from the anus, which he does not have but which he fashioned in men (Arunta has a root *tu*, meaning to hit.).
258. In fact his role seems confined to this; however he performs Intichiuma for all the totems (cf. below, Chapter VIII, section 6).
259. In spite of the evidence, Spencer and Gillen deny that Atnatu has anything in common with Baiame, Daramulun, etc. Cf. *N. T. C.*, pp. 252, 492. On the contrary, it is clear that the tenor of Atnatu's cult is infinitely more religious than that of the cult of the eastern tribes: the myth is completely esoteric, and there is no ceremony reducing Atnatu to the level of the *churinga.*
260. The detail about the chants is not mentioned in the discussion of the meaning of the rites, nor in the résumé, but it is mentioned in the myth: 'the women cease to hear the men singing'. *N. T. C.*, p. 347 [quotation unclear. R.P.]. So we can assume that it is not simply a matter of the sound of the bull-roarers, but also of all the ceremonies and all their chants.
261. *N. T. C.*, p. 499. 'It was when he saw that certain of his sons were not striking the "devils" and were failing to observe the sacred ceremonies in his honour, *for him*, that he threw them to the ground' (a myth which is the opposite of the present sanction: if initiation is not performed regularly according to the rules, Atnatu drags the impious up to the sky).
262. On the oral rites concerning the great gods, see below, Chapter V, initiation rites.
263. On these gods themselves, see below, Book III, Chapter II, 'Myths'.
264. See A.W. Howitt, 'Some Australian Ceremonies of Initiation', J. A. I., XIII, 1884, pp. 432–59, especially p. 457. 'Although there is no worship of Darumulun as, for instance, by prayer'.
265. Cf. below, Chapter V, and Howitt, ibid.: 'yet there is clearly an invocation of him by name'.
266. Howitt, 'Some Australian Ceremonies of Initiation', *J. A. I.* XIII, 1884, p. 454 [page number is spurious. R. P.]; *S. E. A.*, p. 553; cf. pp. 536, 546; 'Notes on Songs and Song Makers', *J. A. I.*, XVI, 1887, pp. 327–35, especially 332; [I have deleted one reference here, because it apparently duplicates what follows. R. P.] cf. 'Some Australian Ceremonies of Initiation', *J. A. I.*, XIII, 1884, p. 555 [page number is spurious. R. P.]; 'Australian Medicine Men', *J. A. I.*, XV, 1887, p. 460 [actually XVI, 1887, pp. 23–59. R. P.]; regarding these synonyms, see below (Chapter V, 2).

267. *S. E. A.*, p. 556.
268. Cf. other cases, below, Chapter IV, Chapter V; on the religious language of gestures and even of ritual objects, see Book III, Chapter IV (relationship between manual rites and oral rites).
269. 'Some Australian Ceremonies of Initiation', p. 450 (this seems to have been known and subsequently confirmed by J. Fraser, *Aborigines of New South Wales*, Sydney, 1892, p. 12), *S. E. A.*, p. 528.
270. *S. E. A.*, p. 586, R. Mathews, 'The Burbung of the Wiradthuri Tribes', *Journal of the Royal Society of New South Wales*, XXIII, 1894, p. 215 [actually XXXI, 1897, p. 111. R. P.]; *J. A. I.*, XXV, 1896, p. 109 [actually 295–318. R. P.], conversely, places these rites among the exoteric rites performed in front of the women when purportedly Dharamulum (who is here a smaller god because he is the son of the great one) takes off the youngsters to initiate them.
271. Taplin, *The Narinyerri Tribe*, p. 55. It is possible, however, that in view of the great number of Narinyerri present, this rite was performed on the occasion of a tribal gathering specifically for an initiation (for these necessary coincidences, see Book III, Chapter IV, 3, 'The feast').
272. See below, Book III. Chapter II, 'Myths'; Taplin, op. cit., p. 57; G. Taplin, *The Folk-lore, Manners, Customs and Languages of the South Australian Aborigines*, Adelaide, 1879, p. 22.
273. Cf. Hubert and Mauss, 'Esquisse d'une théorie générale de la magic', *Année sociologique*, 7, p. 145.
274. Cf. Mauss, 'Origines des pouvoirs magiques', Chapter III.
275. *N. T. C.*, p. 502; cf. p. 501, on the role of Gnabaia in ordinary initiation; on p. 748, it is said that there are three Gnabaias, two hostile and one friendly. Thus the myth would be exactly the same as among the Mara and Binbinga, although the organization of the magic profession is very different.
276. *N. T. C.*, p. 502: 'sings to his Gnabaia'.
277. *N. T. C.*, p. 488. There must be some fault in observing all these documents: Mundadji (p. 487), Mundagadji (p. 501, does not appear in the vocabulary, p. 754), Munkaninji = *munkani* (Mara, Anula, p. 754, spelt *mungurni*, p. 489). All these spirits have strikingly similar names to that of the medicine-man and even the rite (cf. below, the *munguni*, Book III, Chapter II, Sympathetic Magic).
278. We simply cannot understand how Spencer and Gillen were able to state that there is no analogy between the Mara *binbinga* practices and those of the Anula: *N. T. C.*, p. 502.
279. See p. 628. The *munpani* in question is perhaps quite simply *munkani*: a printing error or lack of attention would be enough to explain everything. However, Spencer and Gillen's documents are particularly deficient in logic and philology here.
280. *N. T. C.*, p. 488.

281. Cf. A. W. Howitt, in B. Smyth, *Aborigines of Victoria*, I, p. 473; L. Fison and A.W. Howitt, *Kamilaroi and Kurnai*, London and Melbourne, 1875, p. 220; cf. A. W. Howitt, 'Notes on Songs and Song Makers of some Australian Tribes', *J. A. I.*, XVI, 1887, p. 327, and *S. E. A.*, p. 435. The formula is as follows:

Tundunga Brewinda nundunga mei murriwunda.

'Tundung by Brewin, I believe by the crooked bone, by the eye of the one who threw it'. [The correct page is 437. The text reads: *Tundunga Brewinda nunduunga ugaringa mri-murriwanda. Tundung* by *Brewin* – I believe – hooked by eye of spear-thrower. R.P.] Howitt translated it (*Kamilaroi and Kumai*) as 'O! Tundung!', although he gave the meaning of *Tundung* as fibres of the stringy bark tree. Later on he makes *Tundung* an instrumental, like *Brewinda*. Earlier, in Brough Smyth, he made *Brewinda* a vocative.

282. *S. E. A.*, p. 435. On the subject of the Gournditch Maro, cf. Revd Stähle, in Fison and Howitt, *Kamilaroi and Kurnai*, p. 252, revelation by the dead man of prayers for death, a document which is critically evaluated below, Book III, Chapter II.

283. Brough Smyth, *Aborigines of Victoria*, I, pp. 462–3, cf. *Vocab.* Green *ad verbum*, ibid., II, p. 122. Cf. ibid., a petition to the birds, to which we shall return, Book III, Chapter I, 'Magic rites'.

284. C. S. Ausfeld, 'De Graecorum praecationibus quaestiones.' Suppl. Band XXVIII, *Jahrbuch für Klassische Philologie*, Leipzig, Teubner, 1903, pp. 505ff. Among the noteworthy theses in this work, we draw particular attention to the division into three themes – invocation, the epic part, and prayer, or petition properly so-called.

285. Ibid., p. 506. A curious thing is that the division into *preces rituales* and *preces quae sine actione sacra effunduntur* is not continued in the rest of the work.

286. See our review of Rouse, *Greek Votive Offerings*, in *L'Année sociologique*, VII, 1904, pp. 296–7.

287. Intichiuma of the white cockatoo in the Warramunga, see below.

288. Strehlow, *Die Aranda Stämme*, I, p. 4 and ibid., n.5, actually links the word to the root *inti*, which means to teach. All the ceremonies of the totemic cult would be *intijiuma*, acts of teaching (*intijiuma*, noun, verbal infinitive of the causative of the verb *inti*); consequently, all these ceremonies would come under the totemic ceremonies of initiation. See below, Chapter IV, where we adopt Strehlow's theory in part. But among the *intijiuma*, he distinguishes the *mbatjakuljama* (to put on good terms), which consists of re-establishing good feelings with the totemic gods and inciting the species to reproduce, the rain to fall, etc., which simply

amounts to reinstating the *intichiuma* under another name and giving it a wider and more religious meaning. We would not hesitate to agree with Strehlow if, in general, we did not have a certain mistrust of his etymologies, and if Kempe, 'Vocabulary of the Tribes', *Transactions of the Royal Society of South Australia*, XIV, 2, 1891, p. 93, had not given *intitakerama*, 'to mimic, to speak', which gives a meaning to the radical *inti* not given by Strehlow. See, however, Planert, *Aranda Grammatik*, following Wettengel, pp. 551–66.

289. It is very likely that the Arunta consist of several tribes, and in any case there are certainly several dialects and several rituals (see below); we suspect that the word Intichiuma was used in the sense indicated by the Arunta of the north-east (the Alice Springs group, Tjritja in Arunta, etc. and by neighbouring groups, towards the east.).
290. On these definitions and their accompanying theories, see the references quoted below.
291. According to a rather superficial author, the only tribe in which the powers of the totemic clan have an exclusively positive character is the Piljarri, Paljarri (northern Western Australia), where the members of the clans would have no other power than that of increasing the numbers belonging to their totem; see J. Whitnell, 'Marriage Rites and Relationships', *Australian Anthropological Journal, Science of Man*, 1903, VI, p. 41. But if the fact is plausible, the testimony demands confirmation, because, after all, it is a rather important fact.
292. Thanks to the work of Spencer and Gillen and of the German missionaries: for criticism of their findings, see above.
293. The Arunta were even more numerous around 1874, before the arrival of smallpox, then syphilis and other European diseases (see Schulze, 'Notes on the Aborigines of the Finke River', p. 218. The most powerful of the tribes described by Howitt, the Dieri, numbered 600 at the start of the European occupation; before that, at the time of Gason's census, they had numbered 230 (in Curr, II, p. 44). The very large tribes, like the Wiraidthuri, the Barakunji (3,000 according to Teulon, Curr, II, p. 189) and the Narrinyerri (numbering 3,200 according to Taplin in 1842), are really collections of tribes. Besides, it is very difficult to say where an Australian tribe begins and ends (see below, Book III, part II, conditions of social morphology).
294. Cf. the names of purely geographical origin of the various divisions of the Arunta, Dr E. C. Stirling, *Report of the Horn Expedition*, IV, p. 10. Spencer and Gillen, *N. T.*, p. 9. Even if these names only referred to the divisions of the local groups at the time of the general encampments of the tribe or of its component parts, they would still be of interest. Although they only designate the areas from which the clans come and the way they form encampments according to their original provenance,

perhaps this division is operative within the phratries which determine the organization of the tribal camp here (cf. texts quoted in Durkheim and Mauss, 'Classifications primitives', *L'Année sociologique*, 6, 1903, p. 53. Even if this hypothesis were to be verified, it would simply confirm the supposition that we made at that time).

295. On these dialectal variations, see, for example, Kempe, 'Vocabulary', II, p. 1f.; the variations in the lexicon in particular seem quite important, for example: S.W. *ultunda* (magic stones) = N.E. *atnongara* etc., *Engwura* = *urumpilla.*
296. On these variations, see *N. T., p.* 265. *N. T. C.*, pp. 308–309.
297. On the divisions into 4 and 8 classes, cf. the amusing contradiction between the old missionaries, Kempe and Schulze, *Horn Expedition*, IV, p. 50 and the documents quoted in Durkheim, 'Sur le totémisme', *L'Année sociologique*, 5, p. 82.
298. It emerges from an analysis of Strehlow's documents, *Die Aranda Stämme*, I, p. 3n.5, that the Arunta of the Finke share the entire territory, being divided into eight classes distributed between two phratries, the *Pmalyanuka* and the *Lakakia*. Spencer and Gillen took these proper names to be common nouns: one of them, *nakrakia*, would designate the members of the phratry of the person speaking, the other, *mulyanuka*, that of the opposite phratry. They persisted in this error in their second book, *N. T. C.*
299. There were flourishing stations at Tempe Downs in Loritja country, *Horn Expedition*, IV, p. 7; Schulze, 'Tribes of the Finke River', pp. 220, 229. We refer to the descriptions of the first explorers: W. E. P. Giles, *Australia Twice Traversed*, London, 1889, p. 12 etc., and even those of Spencer and Gillen, *N. T.*, p. 2f. In reality, the Arunta groups do not live in the desert or the steppe except when travelling or pursuing game. However, the country has become one of scattered stations, though it is in fact relatively colonized; cf. R. Mathews, 'Notes on the Languages of Some Tribes of Central Australia', *Journal of the Royal Society of New South Wales*, XXXVIII, p. 420.
300. On hunting, fishing and gathering, see further Spencer and Gillen, *N. T.*, p. 7f.; *N. T. C.*, Schulze, loc. cit., pp. 232–4. [n.300]
301. *N. T. C.*, p. 633f.
302. Cf. below, Book III, part II, 1.
303. The *Engwura* which Spencer and Gillen attended lasted more than three months, during which time the men went out to hunt only exceptionally; cf. 'The Engwura of the Arunta Tribes', *Transactions of the Royal Society of Victoria*, II, pp. 221–3.
304. On the already longstanding degeneration of these tribes, see Schulze, loc. cit., pp. 218 [n.300], 224–5 (changes in social organization). Cf. Kempe, 'Vocabulary', p. 1, on the difficulty of talking to boys who had

not been brought up at the mission. However, we should not deduce from this contradiction that observation, whether by Spencer and Gillen or by other authors, would have been impossible. In the first place, the extreme nomadism of the Arunta preserves them from too strong an influence, in spite of their numerous dealings with Europeans; what is more, it seems that ethnographers and missionaries had the natural prudence not to approach any but very intelligent elders (cf. *N. T. C.*, 'Preface', p. viii and R. Mathews, loc. cit., p. 420); cf. Strehlow, *Die Aranda Stämme*, I, p. 1n.2; cf. fig. 1.

305. Cf. above, also Durkheim, 'Sur le totémisme', *L'Année sociologique*, V, p. 91f.; cf. below, Book III, part II, Chapter II, social conditions. To forestall any criticism at this point, we assume that, at a relatively recent date, the Arunta had an organization similar to that of the Mara and the Anula.
306. Cf. Durkheim, 'Sur l'organisation matrimoniale', *L'Année sociologique*, VIII, p. 124f. In our opinion, at least, the objections raised by N. W. Thomas and A. van Gennep are not valid.
307. A rather little-noticed document by Schulze establishes that the child had two totems, its father's and its mother's, loc. cit., p. 235; cf. p. 238, on the *tmara altjira*, the camp of the Alcheringa, which, according to Schulze, is always the camp of the mother, of the mythical ancestor of the mother; cf. below, Chapter V: totemic ceremonies in the case of loss of blood.
308. Naturally we do not in the least adopt the hypothesis according to which the primitive belief would have been in an entirely miraculous birth, without respect for the totems; for a discussion of the subject, cf. below, Book III, II, I. In any case, to us the question appears to have been rendered void by the simple observation that we would not understand how people would even have arrived at the notion of uterine filiation; cf. *L'Année sociologique*, X, p. 229 [M. Mauss, review of N. W. Thomas, 'The Religious Ideas of the Arunta'; cf. n. 198. R. P.].
309. Except those who are of exactly the same people: Ilpirra, Unmatjera, Kaitish (?) (cf. *N. T. C.*, p. 150f.) and also those who are in a less advanced state of disintegration, since the totems at least remain attached to the phratries. But in the Warramunga and all the tribes of the north, as with the Urabunna and all the tribes of the south, miraculous birth in no way results in an irregular totemic descent.
310. See the list we have provided in 'De quelques formes primitives de classification', *L'Année sociologique*, 6, p. 28n.2, and compare with the following list.
311. Cf. *N. T. C.*, p. 768f. *Arwatja* (small rat); *atjilpa* (the achilpa of *N. T.* wild cat); Bandicoot; *uknulia* (dog); *inarlinga* (ant-eater); *elkuntera* (great white bat); euro; kangaroo; opossum; *untaina* (small rat); *untjipera* (small bat); wallaby; – *arthwarta* (small falcon); *ertwaitja* (bellbird; cf. p. 374, where it is called kupakupalpulu, in a myth); *atnaljulpira* ('grass parrot'); *impi impi*

(small bird), *irkalani* (brown falcon); owl; *atninpiritjira* (parakeet Pr. Alex.); native pheasant; *inturita* (pigeon); *podargus; tulkara* (lark); *taluthalpuna* (wild hen); *thippa-thippa* (small bird); *ertnea* (turkey); *ullakuperra* (small falcon); – snake: brown; *arrikarika; obma* (carpet snake; cf. the generic name for snakes which is in Dieri *womma, apma* Urabunna); *okranina* (non-poisonous), *undathirka* (idem); – lizards: *erliwatjera* (*varanus Gould*); *etjumpa* (*var. sp.*); goama (*var. varius*); *iltjiquara* (*varanus punctatus*); *ilura* (*nephriurius*); Jewish lizard; Parenthie lizard (*var. gigant*) – frog (*lymnodynastes dorsalis*); – fish: *interpitna, irpunga*; – *tjanka* (bulldog ant); *intiliapaiapa* (water beetle); sugar ant; *untjalka* (*unchalqua* in *N. T.* a grub); witchetty grub; – herbaceous grains: *alojantwa, audaua, ingwitjika; injirra; intwuta;* – *elonka* (Marsden's fruit, sp.); (we assume that Spencer and Gillen simply omitted to note the Arunta: *unjiamba* (Hakea flower); *munyera* (the seed of *claytonia balonnensis*); *tjankuna* (a bay); *ultinjkintja, untjirkna* (acacia seeds); *yelka* (bulb of *cyperus rotundus*).

The variant totems are: fire, moon, evening star, stone (? probably tomahawk stone), sun, water (cloud). The wind totem is not mentioned among the irregular totems. A certain number of other totems, which were certainly mentioned in *N. T.*, do not appear in the second volume, for example, *arwarlinga* (a species of Hakea flower), p. 444, *urpura* (magpie), p. 404. The most important of the totems not mentioned in this way is the Akakia plum tree. On the other hand, a good number of totems are spelt, perhaps even named, very differently, for example, *ulira N. T.* p. 439: *ilura N. T. C.*; the serpent *okraina N. T.* p. 342 is called *obma, N. T. C.*; in fact, some of the totems mentioned in *N. T. C.* are missing from the second list, for example *latjia* (the same name as in Strehlow), for a grass seed, p. 731. The number of plant totems is noticeably much greater than in the first list.

A certain number are certainly sub-totems, for example a small grub, *N. T.* p. 301, etc.; cf. below.

312. Strehlow's list of totems. *Die Aranda Stämme*, I (alphabetical order as listed by Planert).

Alkenenera (species of cicada), p. 56n.8; *alknipata* (species of grubs), p. 84; *antana* (opossum), p. 62; *ara, aranga* (kangaroo, the *arunga* of Spencer and Gillen, pp. 2, 6 etc.); *aroa* (euro), pp. 29, 59; *arkara* (a kind of white bird) pp. 67, 73; *arkularkua* (species of cuckoo owl, *Podgardus*), p. 8.

Eritja (*irritcha*, Spencer and Gillen, eagle); pp. 6, 45 etc.; *eroanba* (white crane), p. 76.

Ibara (crane with grey and black stripes), pp. 19, 75, 82; *ibiljakua* (ducks), pp. 11, 74; *ilanga* (small lizard), p. 81; *ilia* (emu, *erlia* in Spencer and Gillen), p. 6, etc; *ilkumba, ilbala* (species of bushes, p. 67; *ilbala* (ilbula? *tea tree*), p. 98; *iltjenna* (crayfish), p. 46n.19, *imbarka* (centipede), Table IV, note 5: *inalanga* (inarlinga of Spencer and Gillen) (echidna), pp. 6, 8 etc.; *injitjera* (frog), p. 52 (cf. *inyalanga* in Spencer and Gillen for the preceding totem and for this one) : *injitjinjitja* (small black birds), p. 91; *injunanga* (larva of the gum tree), pp. 85, 11 (but there is negligence here on the part of Strehlow); *injikantja* (poisoned gum? Giftdrüse?) [venom gland. R. P.]); *intjira* (black lizard), p. 60; *inkaia* (small bandicoot), pp. 66, 76; *inkenikena* (bird of prey, probably a Loritja totem), p. 45; *inkalentja* (small falcon), p. 81; *iwuta* (wallaby), p. 57 (cf. Spencer and Gillen, *N. T. C.*, p. 768; other names of wallaby totems, perhaps of other species, *luta, putaia); irbanga,* (*irpunga,* Spencer and Gillen, fish of all species, one of the rare known generic totems), 46n.19; *irkentera* (bat, Spencer and Gillen, *elkuntera); irkna* or *jelka* (*yelka,* Spencer and Gillen, yams), p. 87.

Ulultara (parrot), p. 78; *ulbatja* (parrot), p. 78; *ulbulbana* (bat), p. 46; *ultamba* (bees), p. 67; *urartja* (rat), p. 46; *urbura* (small bird of the genus of the magpie, *craticus nigricularis* Gould), pp. 2, 19; *urturta) urturba,* table VIII, fig. 2, small falcon), p. 39; *utnea* (species of poisonous snake), p. 48n.2, 18, 94, 28.

Kelupa (long black poisonous snake), pp. 29, 50; *kulaia* (another snake), pp. 78, 57; *kutakuta* (or *kutukutu*, small red nocturnal bird; *kurtakurta* in Spencer and Gillen, *N. T.*, p. 232f., cf. ibid., p. 651 is obviously the same), cf. p. 20, cf. p. 53n.4 (Loritja); *knarinja* (long non-poisonous snake), p. 50; *knulja* (*uknulia* in Spencer and Gillen, N. T. C., p. 768, dogs), 27, cf. 39; *kwaka* (species of *Podargus*), p. 67n.4; *kwalba* (grey marsupial rat), p. 66; *kweba* (another species of the same animal?), p. 78.

Nkebara (cormorant), pp. 46, 74; *ngapa* (crow, *corvus coronoides*), pp. 76, 6; *nganka* (crows,, identical with *ngapa?*), p. 58; *nguratja* (long poisonous snake, p. 29).

Tjilpa (wild cat, Achilpa in Spencer and Gillen), p. 9 etc.; *tjilpara tjilpara* (*thippa thippa* in Spencer and Gillen) (very small bird with green wings and red breast), p. 37; *tjunba* (*varanus giganteus,* giant lizard, *echunpa, etjunpa* in Spencer and Gillen), pp. 6, 79.

Ntjuara (white crane), pp. 8, 90 (another identification);

Pipatja (species of grub), p. 84; *jerramba* (*yarumpa* in Spencer and Gillen, honey ant), p. 82.

Tangatja (larva of ironwood grubs), p. 86; *tantana* (black heron), p. 76; *tekua* (species of rat), p. 46; *terenta* (frog), pp. 81, 99; *tokia* (mouse), p. 46; *tonanga* (edible larva of an ant), Table I, I; *titjeritjera* (shepherd's campion, *Sauloprocta motacilloides*).

Tnalapaltarkna (species of nocturnal heron), p. 76; *tnatata* (scorpion), t. III, p. 2; *tnimatja* (sort of larva which lives on the *tnima* bush), p. 86; *tnunka* (kangaroo rat), pp. 8, 59, 64–65 (*atnunga in* Spencer and Gillen), *tnurungatja* (witchetty grub, *udnirringita* in Spencer and Gillen), p. 84.

Palkanja (martin-fisher, for example: Halcyon spec.), p. 77; *pattatjentja* (mud magpie, small bird of the magpie genus), p. 28; *putaia* (wallaby, alias *luta,* alias *aranga*), pp. 9, 65.

Maia maia (large white larva which lives on bushes of the *udnirringa* type in Spencer and Gillen, *tnurunga* in Strehlow), p. 84; *maljurkarra* (female of marsupial rat?), p. 99; *manga* (flies, generic?), p. 49; *mangarabuntja* (fly men?), pp. 61, 96; *mangarkunyerkunja* (lizard cave flies), p. 6; *manginta* (a species of owl), p. 67; *milkara* (a species of green parrot with a yellow patch on its head, *Calopsitt. Nov. Holl.*), p. 79; *mulkamara* (meat fly), Vol. III, 1; *nbangambaga* (mouse porcupine), p. 86.

Wonkara (species of ducks), p. 2.

Rakara (species of red dove), pp. 10, 67, 69; *cramaia* (species of lizard), p. 80; *raltaralta* (species of small fish, *Nematoccitris tatii*), p. 47n.3; *crenina* (species of snake, four feet long, non-poisonous), p. 48n.2; *rebilanga* (large white bird), p. 73.

Lakabara (black falcon), pp. 8, 97; *lintjalenga* (grey falcon), p. 8; *luta* (species of wallaby), pp. 9, 64; *ltjeljera* (species of lizard reputed to be of dissolute habits, *Iturkawura*, tufted, cf. *nephriurus*, p. 11n.2, cf. Spencer and Gillen, *N. T.* , p. 8 etc.).

The variant totems which Strehlow mentions are water, *kwatia* (*quatcha* in Spencer and Gillen) with its sub-totem, hail, *tnamia* (p. 26); *taia* (the moon), Table II, 2; *latjia*, seeds, p. 76; *ratapa* (*erathipa* in Spencer and Gillen, children), pp. 87, 80, cf. Table IV, 3. This last is a sub-totem of the lizard *ramaia* (in Spencer and Gillen of the lizard *echunpa*), p. 80, or perhaps, in other divisions, an independent totem. However, there are reasons also for the existence of this totem which we will indicate below. Finally comes fire, p. 90.

A good number of these totems seem to us to be sub-totems of the others, see below. This is already obvious in the case of the fly totems; see the list under *manga*, etc.

One can see the great divergence between this list and that of Spencer and Gillen; but we should not argue against their list on this account. In fact the observations relate to parts of the Arunta tribe that are sufficiently far apart for the totems and ranks of sub-totems to be totally different (see Book III, the familial character of mythologies).

313. *N. T.*, p. 9.
314. *N. T.*, p. 169.
315. *N. T.*, pp. 11, 169.
316. *N. T.*, pp. 119, 267; cf. the intichiuma of the rain, below.
317. Cf. *N. T. C.*, preface, p. xiv. These cults even end up resembling those of the confraternities, which we consider to be the case for the witchetty grubs, cf. below; we say confraternity on account of the miraculous nature of recruitment to the clan, which has ceased to be hereditary. *N. T.*, p. 11; cf. below. We have purposely gone into some detail regarding this characteristic of religious organization, so as to show it as it really is: something both very developed and very degenerate, although it has

admirably preserved some very primitive features. Thus we are reacting against the tendency to make the Arunta the purest representatives of Australian civilization, as well as against the opposite view which regards them as the most extreme development of that civilization, while still regarding them as its most typical exponents (on these points, cf. Book III, Chapter I, social conditions). We believe they constitute one of the most singular exceptions among Australian societies. The sort of fascination they exert at present on the science of religions and on sociology proceeds simply from a kind of scientific fashion, as well as from the wealth of documents on them. In a way, this very abundance has distorted in their favour the wise and critical weighing of evidence.

318. For example, the Intichiumas of the Bandicoot, *N. T.*, pp. 205–6 of the long-horned chrysalis, *idnimita*, ibid. p. 206 of the bulb *irriakurra* ibid; of the plum tree *Akakia*, *N. T.*, p. 205 can be assumed, since we know about their totemic sacraments, which can only follow an Intichiuma.
319. The Intichiuma of fire; cf. below; the Intichiuma of rain.
320. Schulze, 'Aborigines of the Finke River,' *Transactions of the Royal Society of South Australia.*, 1891, XII, p. 218.
321. Ibid., p. 221. At that time the missionaries (cf. Kempe, 'Vocabulary', *ad verbum; a corroboree, tjurunga,* to be strong, p. 50), understood perfectly the meaning of the word *tjurunga* (*churiña* in Stirling, *Horn Expedition*, IV, pp. 77–8, *churinga* in Spencer and Gillen) and knew that it designated the sacred, the sacred ceremony, the sacred chant and the *churinga* that were employed there, with whose usage they were completely familiar (cf. Schulze, p. 244). One could say that the confusion that reigned among observers at that time between the Intichiuma and the other *tjurunga* ceremonies was not as far from the truth as the excessively sharp distinction introduced by Spencer and Gillen.
322. Ibid, p. 245.
323. Ibid., p. 241: 'Worship or more correctly idolatrous service'.
324. Ibid., p. 243, visits on behalf of others; pp. 241–2, 244, ownership of the formula and rite.
325. Ibid., pp. 221, 243. Unfortunately, Schulze had not distinguished between the *ildada* corroborees (*althertha* in Spencer and Gillen) and the ceremonies of the totemic cult, so that his description applies to both, although he certainly saw distinct ceremonies, p. 243.
326. Ibid., pp. 243, 221, 244.
327. E.g., from high fa to lah and from there to low mi and then going back to high fa.
328. Ibid., p. 245.
329. It is clear that imitation is only possible in the case of totemic animals. However, we note vocal imitations of the sound of thunder, wind etc. (cf.

below, and Book III, II, Chapter III, the languages of nature), for everything calls out and speaks.

330. See below, in the Intichiuma of the rain, the imitation of the plover.
331. Perhaps Schulze is referring to the cry of the animal when he speaks of the 'monosyllabic' character of the formulae. But he may be thinking not only of animal cries but also of ritual interjections. (Cf. below, Book III, II, Chapter III – ritual conditions – religious interjections.)
332. Ibid., p. 221.
333. In his description, as in the works of Spencer and Gillen, this accounts for the incorrect use of the word burden or refrain to designate the collective repetition of the chant formula. Whenever it is appropriate, we shall indicate those cases where there is a refrain or a choir responding to a soloist.
334. Ibid., pp. 221, 243.
335. Ibid., p. 21; cf. below, Chapter IV, on alliteration in totemic chants.
336. Ibid., pp. 221, 243.
337. Ibid., Formula 4, p. 244; *talenta, terenta* is a suffix of quantity. We draw attention to the metrical balance of the two clauses of the formula, whose last five syllables are identical in sound as in meaning.
338. It can in fact refer to the expression of the wish, but it can also describe a certain quantity of honey represented symbolically by the churinga (cf. in the Intichiuma of the Hakea flower. *N. T.* p. 184, the stone which represents a mass of flowers), or a quantity of honey which existed in the past (cf. below on the multiple meanings of the formula).
339. Ibid., no. 3, p. 244. The formula is obscure and the translation unclear; not only is the bird in question unknown, but neither do we fully understand the translation 'mountain-sized water' because in the expression we recognize *laia*, lake (cf. the lake of souls, pp. 239, 249; cf. Strehlow, *Ar. St.* I, p. 3), *irbmana*, mountain; see Kempe, 'Vocabulary', *ad verbum*; but the form *intji* (auxiliary?) is unknown to us; and the English could be equally well rendered as 'the water which is situated on the mountain' or 'the water which has the dimensions of the mountain'. We adopt the first translation because, in our opinion, the formula alludes to the totemic centre, the 'water hole' in the mountain.
340. Formula 1, p. 243. We do not understand the dative with *titja titja* or with *rama*.
341. Formula 2, p. 247. The dative here is as incomprehensible to us as in the preceding formula. Neither of these formulae is to be foumd in the complete *tjurunga* of the emu, which we shall describe below.
342. Ibid. p. 243. Schulze writes English very badly; so we are sometimes obliged to interpret him. [Mauss's French translation reads as follows in English: In the text the original English has been given. The quotation comes from a paper delivered in German and translated into English by J. G. O. Tepper for the *Transactions*. R.P.]

343. Ibid., p. 244.
344. He is supposed to understand them, through or by original inspiration, p. 242.
345. Ibid., p. 244.
346. We can recognize here all the features of the primitive round (cf. below, Book III, II, end of Chapter IV).
347. Elsewhere Spencer and Gillen mentioned all the conditions for the Intichiuma that Schulze had already noted: they have a direct and particular efficacy and act immediately on the totemic species; they insure its existence and multiplication if it is animal or vegetable, *N. T. C.*, p. 288, *N. T.*, pp. 167–170 (cf. below for a critique of this theory). They belong to a local section of the clan, *N. T.*, p. 11; they vary in each local group, there cannot be two which are identical, *N. T.*, p. 119, *N. T. C.*, p. 267; also the Ulatherka group of the witchetty grubs has a different Intichiuma from the Alice Springs group; they belong more especially to the headman, *alatunja*, p. 11.
348. *N. T.*, pp. 11, 169, *N. T. C.*, pp. 257, 315; cf. 'President's Address', *Australian Association for the Advancement of Science*, 1904, p. 165. On this point of the secret of the Intichiuma among the Arunta and Ilpirra, see below.
349. *N. T.*, loc. cit.; cf. *N. T. C.*, pp. 315–6. On the regularity, see below.
350. The name of the grub, of the insect called witchetty in its grub state (because the Arunta know the animal's life history perfectly), is *udnirringita* (*N. T. C.*, pp. 289–90). According to Spencer and Gillen, it comes from the *udnirringa* shrub where the insect lays its eggs and where the larvae live; cf. Strehlow, *Die Aranda und Loritja Stämme*, I, p. 84, *tnurungatja.*
351. Tjoridja, in Arunta, cf. Strehlow, op. cit., I, 85, p. 41. See below, Chapter IV, a discussion of the nature of the pilgrimage which seems to have preceded the Intichiuma.
352. *N. T.*, pp. 423, 11. The group numbers forty individuals. By right of ownership and by virtue of its mythical descent (each individual being the reincarnation of an ancestor whose double continues to live in the ground), it occupies an area of more than 100 English square miles.
353. *N. T.*, pp. 170, 179; cf. *N. T. C.*, p. 289f.
354. *N. T.* p. 423f.; the myth of the western group of this totem (the Ulaterka-Ulathurqua, Spencer and Gillen) is given by Strehlow, op. cit., I, note 55. He leads the founders of the Ulaterka group precisely to Emily Gap, where they hear Antaljiuka singing (p. 85n.4), while he listens to them.
355. On the *alatunja*, see *N. T.* pp. 65, 153, 166, 169, 119, cf. *N. T. C.*, pp. 25, 188. Strehlow gives another name for the headman *inkata*, op. cit., I, 2, p. 7. Kempe, *Vocabulary*, l. l., p. 42, col 2.
356. *N. T.*, p. 170.

357. *N. T.*, figs. 25, 24, pp. 171, 173, figs. 93, 94, pp. 426–7. The name of the gorge in Arunta is *Unthurqua.* See the description, pp. 424–5 (*inturka,* Strehlow, op. cit., I, p. 84n.9: the belly; the term is highly significant of the reproductive role of this place in the earth).
358. *N. T.*, p. 171.
359. *N. T.*, p. 425.
360. *N. T.*, p. 427.
361. *N. T.*, p. 425.
362. *N. T.*, p. 172, *oknira ilthura* (the great hole, cf. p. 650). *N. T. C.*, p. 267.
363. *N. T.*, p. 652.
364. Cf. *N. T. C., p.* 289. The rite is neglected and the formula not mentioned.
365. *N. T.*, p. 172.
366. *N. T.*, p. 424, and which are called *churinga unchima* (sacred eggs, *churinga eggs;* on the *churinga,* cf. below, Chapter V conclusions; cf. Book III, Part II, Chapter II, ritual conditions). Here we are passing over a rite which contains a formula: the *alatunja* takes each of these stones and, striking the stomach of each of the participants, says: *Unga murna okirra* (wrongly written elsewhere as *oknira*) *ulkinna* 'You (thou, cf. Strehlow, Planert, *unta*) have eaten a lot (*knira,* Strehlow) of food'. This ceremony is in fact a complex rite, and we shall return to it (Book III, Part II, Chapter III, mental states): it is a simple ritual formula descriptive of a departure rite (for here we have the *atnita ulpilima,* the relaxation of the intestines which had been knotted with religious emotion; cf. *N. T.*, pp. 182, 184), which closes the first part of the whole ritual; but it has probably become an efficacious formula (an imitation of females becoming pregnant? an imitation of the repletion of the stomach after a feast?).
367. *N. T.*, pp. 425, 430.
368. *N. T.*, p. 426; cf. p. 172 'decorated eyes'. The first translation is not as good as the second, 'eyes painted around'. What is certain is the meaning of the word *alkna,* eye. Fig. 132, p. 632, seems to be a precise reproduction of this painting.
369. Spencer and Gillen attach so little importance to these formulae, which are in fact so interesting, that they do not mention them in their résumé (*N. T. C.*, p. 290).
370. *N. T.*, p. 427.
371. This point in the ritual is given due note only in *N. T. C.*, p. 290.
372. *Churinga uchaqua, N. T.*, p. 173. Is the polishing of the *churinga* applicable only to the cult of the grub's egg, or is it also a sort of unction poured over the body of the ancestor? We do not know. Perhaps it has both meanings.
373. Are these responses to that of the *alatunja,* or the same chants repeated in chorus?
374. Cf. above.

375. *N. T., p.* 431. The very name of Intwailjuka, Antaljiuka (Strehlow) means 'that he was on the look-out and listening' (the chants); Strehlow, op. cit., I, p. 84n.4.
376. On the device, see below, III, Parts II, III, ritual conditions.
377. This rite probably consists of: an imitation of the sound of the flight of the insect, perhaps of the flight itself; a cult of the bush that gives its name to the insect; an invitation to the insects to go and reproduce on all the bushes of the same species.
378. We are evidently dealing here with those who belong to other totems and are wearing their own decorations on this day.
379. *N. T.*, p. 176. The meaning is not given, but the metrical form is very clear except in the third line. It is possible that this is no more than a formula of greeting: *ilkna*, cf. *ilknia*, totemic design (greeting to the decorated people!?). *Yaalan* = *jala* (Strehlow), yes: *lai* (imperative of *la*, to go?).
380. *N. T.*, p. 178.
381. Ibid.
382. Cf. above.
383. *N. T.*, p. 178.
384. Cf. below, Book III, Part I, Chapter III, *The ritual formula.*
385. Rites of the *ilthura oknira*, etc., above.
386. Texts quoted above.
387. Texts quoted above.
388. Cf. *N. T.*, p. 173, 'low, monotonous chant'.
389. See texts quoted above.
390. See above.
391. See texts quoted above.
392. On this effect, see below, Book III, II, Chapter IV.
393. We cannot express ourselves in any other way than by placing an article in front of the word totem. But this is an imprecise manner of speaking, for the expression 'the totem' represents several things: associated animals in their diverse forms, the great ancestor, other ancestors, the souls of the dead, the doubles of the individuals present, the seeds of souls of future individuals, human and animal. The absence of any article in Australian languages and in general in languages where totemism exists leads precisely to this constant confusion, which it would be imprudent to lose sight of (cf. below, Book III, Part II, Chapter II, mental states).
394. The word invitation in Spencer and Gillen should not be taken in this sense. *N. T.*, p. 172.
395. On this essential notion of totemism, of the way the animal species concedes its body, see below. There is a splendid expression of the notion in a Zuñi myth; see *Mélanges d'histoire des religions*, p. 12n.3.
396. On the totemic sacrament, see below, Chapter V, 4.

397. On the ritual drama identical to the Intichiuma, see Chapter V, conclusion.
398. On the instability of the species, cf. *N. T.*, pp. 520–1. When the animals appear out of season, it is because the *iruntarinia*, the souls (of the dead and of the totem), have themselves performed the Intichiuma.
399. *N. T.*, p. 430.
400. *N. T.*, pp. 43–2; cf. *N. T.*, p. 156.
401. On this quality of time of the *alcheringa*, cf. *N. T.*, p. 387, *N. T. C.*, p. 438; cf. below, Book III, Part II, Chapter II.
402. Cf. *N. T.*, p. 432.
403. See the example below. We consider it extremely likely that one of the reasons for these deviations from normal usage is that they are often obligatory right from the start. As all these formulae are sung, the chant naturally alters the words, especially if it contains variations on a theme.
404. This is how Spencer and Gillen generally interpret them, *N. T.*, pp. 172, 177; cf. below. But they exaggerated the incomprehensibility of the formulae, either because they were ill-informed by Aruntas who had a poor knowledge of the words of the ritual, or because they did not pursue their enquiries sufficiently to learn the secrets of the archaising and archaic language used by the actors of the rites, the language spoken by the ancestors of the *Alcheringa*.
405. Those who themselves have *churinga* names are *churinga*; cf. *N. T., p.* 155; cf. *N. T.*, Chapter VIII; cf. p. 637, the confusion of *churinga* with *nanja*.
406. Cf. texts above.
407. The *churinga* is believed to speak; cf. below, cf. *N. T.*, p. 436.
408. Cf. Strehlow on Thomas, 'The Religious Ideas of the Aruntas', p. 430, Strehlow, *Die Aranda und Loritja Stämme*, I, p. 5.
409. *Okalpara* in Spencer and Gillen, *N. T.*, p. 524, a word incorrectly taken to be the proper name of a specific cave [cannot trace. R.P.]; *ralpara;* Strehlow, op. cit., 5n.3, *kalpara*, p. 8.
410. The idea of their red colour is probably connected with the colour of the ochre with which the re-buried *churinga* are coated.
411. Cf. Strehlow, *Die Aranda Stämme*, I, p. 31 etc.; *ngantja* = the *nanja* of Spencer and Gillen; cf. the Kadimarkara Dieri, below, para. III.
412. Cf. Thomas, 'The Religious Ideas of the Aruntas', p. 430; Strehlow, *Die Aranda Stämme*, I, p. 5; *N. T.*, p. 516.
413. Cf. Spencer and Gillen, *N. T.*, p. 531.
414. Strehlow, *Die Aranda Stämme*, I, p. 28, notes... [apparently unfinished footnote. R. P.]
415. On the propagation of the species through totemic ceremony, see below, Chapter V, conclusion.
416. *N. T.*, pp. 519, 522.

Mauss's Review of Segond's Book on Prayer

SEGOND (J.) – *La Prière* – Essai de psychologie religieuse, Paris, F. Alcan, 1911, 361p.

L'Année sociologique, 12, 1913:239–40.

As M. Segond's essay takes a serious view of our work, we should not disregard it. However, he makes no contribution to the theory of prayer as a religious and social phenomenon. The less said the better about the very long chapter entitled, Collective and Ritual Prayer. Besides appearing to be a digression, appended in the form of an additional note, it fails to meet the demands of criticism. In order to treat such a vast subject, it is not enough to have read a certain number of text-books on the history of religions and the *Année sociologique*. The conclusion of this chapter is that collective prayer, like individual prayer, includes the sense of 'communion'. This must be understood as 'religious sense of a *Presence*' (p.294). The whole question is: what is present? The mystical terms favoured by the author, opposites such as 'definite' and 'indefinite', 'identical or superior to the soul', 'subconscious to the deep self' can be useful enough. But how much more philosophical was the attitude of a St Thomas or a Bossuet, who having adopted a system of ontology, and acknowledging the existence of mystery once and for all, followed thereafter the straight paths of reason and historical observation!

Without questioning the possibility of a sociological study of prayer, M. Segond complains that such a study cannot comprehend anything but externals, and fails to address the problem of the value of prayer, its reality in experience. This is a failure to understand what we are trying to do. Value judgments are the very object of our science: they constitute the matter which sociology seeks to analyse and explain. What makes prayer efficacious is its intimate and profound action on consciousness: these are the problems addressed by the sociologist.

M. Segond's work includes some useful information about certain elements that Christian mystics of the last centuries have recognised as inherent in the life of prayer – recollection, aspiration, self-abandonment, etc.

M. M.

Some Concluding Anthropological Reflections

Howard Morphy

Mauss's unfinished work on prayer – an attempted dissertation that stayed with him much of his life – provokes and puzzles the reader's imagination. Mauss may have lacked a little in self-discipline as his uncle Durkheim suggested, he may also have been at times overburdened by the tasks that Durkheim set him (see Introduction). However, other factors were also at play. The research on prayer can be seen to exist at the point of two paradigm shifts, and times of paradigm change are always periods of uncertainty as well as of conviction. The works of Durkheim and others associated with the *Année sociologique* were central to theoretical developments in both sociology and anthropology. These shifted any explanation away from a simple base fixed on evolutionary models and towards an understanding of phenomena in the context of the societies in which they occurred. Simultaneously a revolution was taking place in ethnographic method. Until the late nineteenth century, missionaries, traders and government officials had collected, in a piecemeal way, facts about other cultures that provided the basis for the construction of theories. Then, in particular in America and Australia, there was a shift towards longer term, more systematic field-work, by trained observers – scientists such as Franz Boas and Baldwin Spencer; and missionaries such as Maurice Leenhardt. One consequence of the changes then taking place was that new topics of research were beginning to emerge just at the time that knowledge of different cultures was increasing exponentially.

In opening up the sociology of religion, Durkheim, Mauss, Hertz and Hubert began to interrogate from a perspective of evolutionary sociology a whole range of topics, such as prayer, that fell under the more general rubric of religion. Their methodology required that they looked at the present through the lens of past societies in order to avoid the analysis being pre-formed by contemporary concepts and presuppositions. It was necessary that sociologists could identify the more general structures and ideas that underaid contemporary practices. And in analysing religion, the ethnography from Australia was destined to play a central role. Yet almost at the very moment at which Mauss turned to the topic, the evidence was transformed through the researches of Spencer and Gillen, and subsequently those of Carl Strehlow. This comes across clearly when Mauss writes 'It is not that all the facts are known, nor are all the known facts well known. We still need to be prepared for some surprises, such as that occasioned by the appearance of the first book by Spencer and Gillen. Some scholars have yet to recover from it, and remain so to speak, fascinated by the Arunta.' (p .66)

Spencer and Gillen's book, *The Native Tribes of Central Australia*, appeared in 1899, almost certainly after Mauss's thesis had taken its initial shape. Further shocks were to follow with the publication of Carl Strehlow's material, which complemented that of Spencer and Gillen and at the same time challenged some of their conclusions. While Durkheim steered his way confidently through any contradictions in the ethnography, Mauss seems to have been more disturbed by them. One reason for this difference may be that an analysis of prayer required a different kind of data from that needed for the more general analysis of religion with which Durkheim was concerned. Ideally the study of prayer calls for transcriptions and translations of oral performances of chants, of praise songs, incantations and so on. Spencer and Gillen's work provided some examples but the examples were few and poorly translated. The oral record was little represented compared with the rich descriptions of ritual performance dance and visual representations. Ironically it was the richness of Spencer and Gillen's descriptions of ritual performance, in particular the ceremony performed at Emily Gap associated with the maintenance of witchetty grubs, that seems to have convinced Mauss that the corpus of Arrernte* oral chants comprise an 'incomparably rich breviary despite its simple exterior'. But the poverty of the oral record unquestionably reduces the depth of his analysis of Arrernte and Australian prayers in general. Nonetheless Mauss's analysis is interesting both in theoretical terms and for the insights he shows into Aboriginal religion, which in some areas anticipate subsequent analysis.

My reflections on Mauss's work will begin by reviewing his arguments in relation to anthropological analysis, before turning to consider how his arguments stand up in the light of more contemporary ethnography. Interestingly, prayer remains as little a used concept in the analysis of Aboriginal religions today as it did when Mauss first turned to the topic. Indeed, the references available to the contemporary researcher are almost identical to

---

* The new English spelling of Arunta, which is used throughout this chapter.

those of a hundred years ago! Yet the data on which an analysis of prayer could be based has greatly increased. While translations of Indigenous song texts and oral performances are still inadequate, the work of T. G. H. Strehlow and R. M. and C. H. Berndt has greatly improved the situation.

Mauss's analysis

Mauss's own opening remarks almost suggest that prayer is all things to all people:

> Infinitely supple, it has taken the most varied forms, by turns adoring and coercive, humble and threatening, dry and full of imagery, immutable and variable, mechanical and mental. It has filled the most varied roles: here it is a brusque demand, there an order, elsewhere a contract, an act of faith, a confession, a supplication, an act of praise, a hosanna (p. 2).'

Mauss's problem is to convert the diversity of 'western' conceptions of prayer into an evolutionary sequence in which the complexity is seen to accrue over time. Yet of course the diversity of western forms also represents competing theological positions in which the nature of prayer is a contested subject.

Mauss adopts a strongly evolutionary approach in which the phenomenon under consideration developed in complexity and diversity over time. He criticises Tylor on the basis that he 'imagined that people started out with the concept of personalities that were at once spiritual and divine – a concept which, in our opinion, is a late idea, fostered precisely by the earliest forms of prayer' (p. 62). This has two opposed consequences. On the one hand his approach is more inclusive in that in effect he develops a broad and encompassing definition which includes both the most elementary and the most advanced forms of a particular phenomenon. On the other, it is distancing in that certain societies' forms of prayers are seen to be evolutionally prior to others. By way of contrast, Fraserian and Tylorian evolutionism, with its narrower definitions, segregated societies on the basis of the presence or absence of religion. The evolutionists, Mauss argues, shared a similar definition with that of the missionaries. For them,

> Christian prayer, or at least prayer conceived as a spiritual interchange between the believer and his God, is the basic model of prayer. Under the influence of this prejudice, they were unable to recognize the common ground between such a concept of prayer and the sort of words which the Australian addresses to his sacred domestic spirits. It is, moreover, for the same reason that Spencer and Gillen refuse to see, in the system of rites and totemic beliefs, a religion properly so-called. So their negative conclusion, in the case in point, lacks the authority usually associated with their testimony. In order to discover

> prayer in Australia, we need to reduce it to its essential elements and to learn how to avoid seeing all religious matters through Christian eyes. (p. 73)

In this final sentence we can see evolutionism and cultural relativism combined in a way characteristic of the Durkheimean school. The concept under investigation almost escapes for a while its Eurocentric entrapment; it ceases to be an index of European civilisation or to be viewed purely through Christian eyes. Yet its freedom is partly illusory. Mauss's comparative analysis is based on the presupposition that since prayer exists in many contemporary complex societies it must have evolved from a more primitive form, and his objective is to discover this more primitive or elementary form. Mauss's approach is indeed based on an evolutionary assumption that a cultural semantic primitive, out of which more complex practices have developed, can be identified and defined.

While it is clearly appropriate to address the problem in terms of cross-cultural categories and try to shift the core meaning of a concept away from its application in contemporaneous European discourse, this does not mean that the concept which is developed applies equally in all cases. To an extent Mauss's cross-cultural categories are *a priori* rather than analytical, since the diversity of the phenomena does not 'change its nature'. Yet where does its nature come from? The centrality of prayer may reflect nothing more than the centrality of prayer in European religious discourse, though in Mauss's case it may also be influenced by his understanding of Indian religions. In interrogating the usefulness of concepts in cross-cultural analysis the anthropologist has to be open to the possibility that in some cases the European concepts have limited salience. The fact that in the Australian Aboriginal context, prayer has seldom been used as an interpretative or analytical concept, suggests that it may be of limited use in interpreting Aboriginal religion. However the absence of the use of the term may not be decisive grounds for its lack of salience; and it is productive to examine possible explanations. The diversity and ambiguity of its usage and meanings may have made it difficult to apply. Its centrality to Christian discourse may have made it less neutral for cross-cultural analysis and its dependence on language may have made it less accessible to short-term observers.

Mauss emphasizes the linguistic dimension of prayer and argues that although in many cases it may have been emptied of meaning by being reduced to a repetitive formula, it is 'always to some extent a *Credo*' (p. 22); 'in prayer the faithful both act and think'. Indeed Mauss treats prayer almost as a form of exegesis, and as a form of exegesis it has a privileged status in the interpretation and understanding of religious behaviour. In prayer 'the demands of language are such that often the prayer itself will specify the precise circumstances and motives which give rise to it.' (pp. 3–4) To Mauss myth and ritual are mutually reinforcing, standing in a relationship of idea to action. He criticises the separation of rites and myths in the history of religion and argues that 'we have scarcely begun to study these phenomena in which cognition (*représentation*) and action are intimately connected, and whose analysis can be so fruitful. Prayer is precisely one of those phenomena where ritual is joined to belief.' (p. 22) However his analytic perspective slips into a theory about religious action in which he assumes that that which is necessary for him to interpret ritual action is necessary for the actors themselves; if the actors are unaware of the meaning of their actions then how can those actions be meaningful to them. Prayers become 'formulae which have lost all meaning'. To Mauss the opposition between myth and ritual is a false one. The attempts to prove that one is evolutionally prior to the other are doomed to failure since idea (as notion and belief) and action are both necessary. Prayer, since it is a form of ritual based on language, inevitably contains both. In prayer myth and ritual 'appear simultaneously and are inseparable ... There can be no question of attributing any sort of primacy to one or to the other' (p. 23).

Mauss's own theory argues for an increasingly prominent role for prayer in religious practice as part of the evolutionary process of religions: 'prayer has been the remarkable tree which, having grown up in the shade of other trees, has ended up smothering them under its vast branches' (p. 23). Mauss's perspective on the evolution of religion shows close parallels to that which Durkheim (see 1912a) was developing, based on the same ethnographic data. Religion evolved from a collective, rite-based practice, closely associated with the collective identity of the group, to more individual based and reflective practices 'less dependent on social causes'. Simultaneously religious action moves over time from mechanical agency to cerebral contemplation; '[prayer] ended up by being no more than thought and an outpouring of the spirit'(p. 6).

Mauss sees in prayer an indissoluble link between idea and action, but he also sees it following an evolutionary sequence which leads from prayers that are more like rites to prayers that are more like myths. The fact that they are indissolubly interlinked becomes almost an assertion. His evolutionary speculation in the end turns in on itself since he sees the precursor of 'fixed and specific forms [of prayer]' as 'requests addressed to a divine or at least spiritual person.' The earliest and most evolved forms of prayer are individual oral rites, as he argued in Australian medicine men.

Unquestionably in Mauss we see clearly stated a method of cross-cultural research in which he tries to develop ideas and arguments independent of the presuppositions of his own cultural milieu. In criticising the theories developed by philosophers and theologians he argues that their 'whole progression of ideas ... is dominated by the mental state of these authors.' The process of defining is part of an analytic process in which the meaning of the analytical or substantive term defined changes as a result of the research process. The process is one of dialogue and the definition may only emerge at the end of the process.

> There is no question, of course, of defining the very substance of the facts straight away. Such a definition can come only at the end of our study: the one we must make at the beginning can be only provisional. It is meant simply to stimulate research ... without anticipating its results' (p. 37).

Later on he goes on to argue that:

> While we are seeking to establish this idea of prayer, we are in no way bound by current ideas; nevertheless, we should not do needless violence to those ideas. It is certainly not a question of giving a totally new meaning to a word in common use, but of replacing the usual, confused concept with a clearer and more distinct one (p. 49).

It is interesting, however, that in his general argument he leaves the individualistic prayers of the liberal Protestants, which are the highest forms of prayer, far behind. Prayer in its essence is seen as a social phenomenon whose meaning lies partly in its history. In his analysis of *in nomine patris* he concludes that

> A prayer is not just the effusion of a soul, a cry which expresses a feeling. It is a fragment of a religion. In it one can hear the echo of numberless phrases; it is a tiny piece of literature, it is the product of the accumulated efforts of men and women, over generations (p. 33).

And it is to noted here that he reinterprets the prayers of the liberal Protestants by seeing the Spirit to whom they abandon themselves to be in fact the product of the teachings and moral doctrines of their church. He argues that in the highest forms of religion collective prayer is further transformed into a ritual act by being restricted to a prayer book and the 'circumstances, time and place where the prayer should be said, the required posture, all these are strictly laid down' (p. 34). The social nature of the definition emerges strongly in which 'all prayer is a ritual form of speech adopted by a religious society'. It is almost as if the highest form of prayer of the liberal Protestant has escaped the definition altogether or is in fact redefined as a far less individualistic act: 'the individual is borrowing a language he did not invent'. Indeed Mauss argues that if we came across religious acts which were prayer-like in some respects but showed no trace of conformism, such an essential difference would oblige us to classify them separately and give them a different name.

Mauss's argument interestingly becomes one of *langue* versus *parole*, the relationship of the individual to society: 'Instead of seeing in individual prayer the principle behind collective prayer, we are making the latter the principle behind the former. Thus we avoid the error of deriving the complex from the simple'. (p. 36) This of course leaves the apparent contradiction of the individual prayer of the liberal Protestants as being the highest form of prayer and hence the need for them to be speaking in 'a language they did not invent'.

There is a contradiction between his evolutionary perspective and his use of theory to analyse particular cases. Significantly it is the latter that influenced the course of social anthropology: 'there is a necessary link between a given prayer, a given society and a given religion.' Prayer is linked both to the general form of the society and to the religious sphere as a whole. Thus elementary forms of the prayer will be linked to the organisation of the clan. But prayer will also differ according to whether 'mythical powers are personified or not, and whether there is a priesthood or not' (p. 46), though these in turn are strongly influenced by the social milieu. That contradiction may explain his difficulties in this book in that the very method of analysis he adopts undermines the evolutionary argument that he develops. Indeed he hints at this when he writes that 'prayer, as we have seen, is in a constant state of development. It would be difficult to fix a moment at which it is more fully realized than any other time.' (p. 43)

The definition of prayer that Mauss develops in the end manages both to constrain the limits of Protestant individualism by emphasising tradition and the ritual context, and to separate prayer from magic acts by insisting on its reference to the sacred. Prayer is seen as a particular kind of religious rite and hence is dependent on the prior definition of rites. To Mauss *religious rites are efficacious, traditional actions which bear on sacred things* and *prayer is a religious rite which is oral and has direct bearing on sacred things.* Prayer is a collective ritual act and one that is always efficacious; even if the main focus of the prayer appears to be adoration of the powers it is 'still efficacious because it causes the God to act in a certain way.' He differentiates it from incantation on the grounds that incantation need not make reference to any force outside itself. Prayer is any 'text which mentions a religious power' though of course some prayers are incantations and some incantations are prayers! It may indeed be that they have been differentiated on a quite different basis: prayer is a means of acting on sacred things.

Prayer and Aboriginal religion

Mauss bases his analysis initially on the ethnography of the Australian Aborigines, though in the final work they would only have been a beginning. He adopts this approach on theoretical and methodological grounds. He does so partly to shift focus away from contemporary concepts of prayer which may have developed in ways which obscure the origins of the practice and which might even mask core aspects of the concept. However he believes that the Australian data is appropriate because it illustrates aspects of the progressive development of prayer as it articulates with other religious phenomena:

> They will help us look in the right place to discover the laws of an evolution ... even if there is considerable distance between Australian oral practices and even those of ancient religions, there have existed and continue to exist logical connections between the two sorts of ritual (p. 74).

Australian prayer is incorporated within ritual practice through its close links with the totemic system which is the most archaic religious system hitherto discovered by history and ethnography (p. 67).

Mauss reviews the references to prayer among the Australian Aborigines and concludes that the viewpoints can be neatly divided in two: a minority of writers including Langloh Parker argue that Aborigines have prayer and the remainder including Curr, Howitt and Spencer and Gillen argue that they do not. His review of the literature seems at times to be a desperate quest for the evidence of prayer, and at times the reader might be justified in doubting that he will find it. This is mainly because, despite his more general definition, Mauss's conception of prayer is that in its most developed form it is completely mental and interior. In this he shows some sympathy with liberal Protestants. The implicit distinction that he draws between ritual and magic means that the more selfless, less demanding, and less magical the practice the more it shares the attributes of prayer.

The most elementary forms of prayer are ones in which the performers demand action from the totemic powers or move them into action through the power of their invocations. The higher forms of prayer are more supplicatory and increasingly form part of an abstract individual dialogue with God. The highest forms are rarely glimpsed and the early ethnography he cites is subjected to rigorous examination. Almost grudgingly he writes: 'one can perceive, not only the mass of forms that are elementary, confused and complex, but also faint outlines and beginnings, attempts at a more finished mode of expression'. (p. 73)

Of those using the oral rites it is the medicine men who come closest to prayer. Mauss wonders how an institution that is so central to the evolution of religion can owe so much to medicine men, whom he presumably associates with magic and demonstrably false beliefs. His answer is that they often draw upon the cleverest men of society and hence must have the intellect to provide the exegesis on ritual behaviour. But he also argues that they are the agents of progress.

The borderline between religion and magic is a continuing problem to Mauss in his review of the data since both are expressions of desire. He finds elements of prayer strongly present in the incantations associated with rain-making: 'the rites obviously express the desire, the need and the moral and material distress of a whole group of people.' The words are easily understood as a sort of prayer [and here he equivocates] or wish. (p. 74) Typically in this discussion he is edging towards a definition of the invocations of the rainmakers as prayer, before backing off and seeking to delimit the sense in which they are prayers.

Writing about a ceremony that Bunce records in which people of the Geelong area tried to ward off a storm, he questions whether their words were of a precatory character. Indeed 'when the storm fails to abate they exclaimed Marmingatha is very sullen: why?' and 'spat into the air in the direction of the storm.' Mauss concludes from this that words first uttered were more likely to be in the form of orders rather than signs of respect for a spiritual personage, since when they failed, Marmingatha was exposed to insults.

Mauss then examines a number of cases in which people call out the names of their totemic familiars, in some cases to provide generalised protection or warning against danger, in other cases to facilitate success in hunting. In the first two cases he examines the 'rite' that takes place during the evening before going to sleep, and one is tempted to see Mauss being influenced by the analogy with evening prayers in a Christian context. The difference between some of these practices – for example, the ones that bring success in hunting – and rain making seem minimal. And again he states: 'there is a very fine line between invocation and evocation, even magical evocation.' And he concludes, having said that they have the principal characteristics of prayer, that 'the high point reached by these formulae of totemic ritual in their tendency towards other types of prayer, is neither really stable nor very elevated'(p. 77). The names and gestures evoke rather than invoke the God and they 'express in the most summary phraseology that the divinity is far off and that one wishes to make the divinity draw near'. (p. 79)

Mauss at this point turns to look for prayer in the ritual context and at the same time begins to pay more attention to the form of the prayer. He notes that only the most developed form of prayer can be analysed as a literary text and even then he thinks it is better to analyse it in the context of use. Incantations that occur in a religious context are almost pre-defined as prayer. Citing Schulze, a missionary who worked among the Arrernte, Mauss is able to assert the religious nature of the ceremony. The sacred songs and objects are noted to be the property of the clan not of the individual, and the performance is collective in character. In this final section the shift in interpretation is most dramatic as he moves from an almost dismissive view of the language of Aboriginal ritual to a more complex and sympathetic view. Yet even in his dismissive mode he is interesting.

Again following Schulze he notes:

> But sometimes the oral rite can be nothing more than a simple cry, the cry of the animal being represented; we have already seen examples of this custom in the calls addressed to the totem. In this case it is even more clearly a mere gesture, a rhythmic sound, either imitating, as here, the natural rhythm of a bird song, or repeated at regular intervals, separated by pauses, with a single steady beat. ... The cry is necessarily monotonous. It is

> repeated indefinitely: it ends by being a sort of vocal habit. Even the modulation ceases to be free: variations are impossible (p. 88).

However, he goes on 'one should not exaggerate too much the difference between this cry and the formula'. It is tempting to see this cry in Mauss's imagination as a primal scream, or a contentless yearning for spiritual attachment, that signifies the beginning of the religious experience but arguably connects to later expressions of prayer, even to 'the effusion of the soul' of the liberal Protestants. The idea of form emerging from the formless, the complex from the simple also connects with an earlier evolutionary theory. It is almost Pitt-Riversian in its concept.

Mauss goes on to dwell on the monotony of Aboriginal musical performance. Citing Schulze again, he states that the formulae are no more than four or five words strung together according to the poor syntax of such languages. It is a child-like expression of intense desire and hoped for satisfaction. However he then goes on to look at the significance of the chant from a quite different perspective – evoking the presence of a past world of plenty – and he concludes 'there is a constant, easy and immediate passage from the mythical past to the ritual future'.

Once more citing Schulze he stresses the 'obscurity and unintelligibility' of many of the formulae. But he is unsatisfied with Schulze's data: there is nothing but 'the collective, banal, stereotyped and mechanical' corresponding to material need. If that is all, he asks, how could all other forms of prayer have grown out of it? It is here that the turns to Spencer and Gillen and to Strehlow to lead him back to the more advanced forms.

Mauss uses Spencer and Gillen's (1899) account of the ceremony for the witchetty grub at Emily Gap, an immensely rich description of a complex rite which provokes other analogies with Christian practice. The journey from site to site along the path of the ancestral grubs is similar to the way a pilgrimage goes in procession to the various places where a saint is commemorated. The chanting that occurs is seen as a liturgy. The description is immensely powerful and resonates with religious imagery and it is tempting to argue that Mauss had to find prayer there in its more developed form, since, as Pickering argues in the introduction, prayer to Mauss comes close to marking the origins of religion. Yet the prayers themselves remain:

> monotonous rhythmic chants attached to bodily rites ... They contain sentiments and ideas that are in no way individual, but merely crude and stark expressions of needs and expectations ... It is hard to imagine any activity more forcefully obstinate than this endless repetition, for forty-eight hours of unpoetical sentences, of uniform musical themes, in short, of chants which are of little artistic merit and quite without appeal to the emotions (p. 94).

However, he again changes direction by identifying a number of themes 'which run through this apparently shapeless mass of short magico-religious ballads. This makes it into an incomparably rich breviary despite its simple exterior'. (p. 94)

This switch is nowhere more apparent than in the change of value attributed to the unintelligibility of the words; their very difference from ordinary language, the very restrictedness of knowledge of their meanings, enhances their spiritual value.

'The chant not straightforwardly merely the expression of the wishes of the ritual actors ... It is of higher origin, possesses greater inner merit and dignity'. (p. 95) The language is the language of the ancestors but also becomes the language of the postulants, 'the formula is a means of reviving the mythical ancestors who live in the stones'. The songs in turn have a real effect on the participants: 'In the same way as erotic songs act on human desires, so the formulae prompt beings, animal, men and gods, revitalised by the spoken words of the rite, to the prosperous fulfilment of their destiny.' (p. 96) The efficacy however is reinforced by the fact that in the annual cycle the grubs do appear to reproduce themselves.

It is at this point, where the analysis of the use of formulae (ritual incantations) in Arrernte ceremony seems to have provided decisive evidence for the existence of prayer that Mauss ends his text.

Prayer in the study of Aboriginal religion: a continuing absence?

While no one can definitely say why Mauss gave up his dissertation at the point at which he was half way through his analysis of the Arrernte material, it may simply be that the uncertainty of the project eventually proved too much. When he began his research on prayer he had at his disposal relatively limited ethnographic resources that conveyed a partial and impoverished account of Aboriginal society and religion. As he continued his research the picture became richer and the writings of Spencer and Gillen provided strong evidence for religious practice in Central Australian society, evidence that formed the basis of Durkheim's ethnography in *The Elementary Forms of the Religious Life* (1912a). Yet Spencer and Gillen's data on the oral rites were limited and Carl Strehlow's criticisms cast doubt on their understanding of song language. While the new evidence made an even stronger case for the existence of prayer it may have made redundant much of the earlier argument that squeezed evidence out of impoverished ethnography. It may even have begun to make the Arrernte too evolved! Some support for this point of view is provided by almost the last footnote that Mauss wrote:

> [Spencer and Gillen] exaggerated the incomprehensibility of the formulae, either because they were ill-informed by Aruntas who had a poor knowledge of the words of the ritual; or because they did not pursue their enquiries sufficiently to learn the secrets of the archaising and archaic language used by the actors of the rites, the language spoken by the ancestors of the *Alcheringa* (note 405).

While Spencer and Gillen's work has stood up well in the light of subsequent research there is no question that the richness of Indigenous oral performances, songs, chants, incantations of power names was, and remains, poorly represented in the literature. While the multi-valent, subtle and poetic nature of Aboriginal song-poetry has long been taken into account in analyses of Aboriginal religion and society by writers such as Keen (1996), Magowan (2001), Morphy (1986, 1991), and Williams (1986), there have been few studies specifically directed to the topic. Ronald and Catherine Berndt produced many works based on the translation of song texts (see for example Berndt 1952). While these translations in general reflect well the content of the song series and provide an invaluable resource for subsequent analysis, they are interpretative translations and are not generally accompanied by interlinear translations of the texts. Indeed T. G. H Strehlow's magisterial work *Songs of Central Australia* published in 1971 remains unique in providing a detailed analysis of Aboriginal song texts. The son of the missionary Carl Strehlow, T. G. H. Strehlow's transcriptions are of Arrernte songs and had they been available 70 years earlier would have significantly altered Mauss understandings.

Strehlow challenged the view that songs were merely a collection of sounds that cannot be translated (1971:9). He acknowledged however that the songs were difficult to translate partly because the 'rhythmic measure not merely changes the prose accentuations of individual words – it also reshapes the form of the words of which the line is composed' (ibid.:64). His data both demonstrate the complexity of Arrernte songs and also support some of the conclusions of earlier researchers. Strehlow agrees that some of the phonetic differences between the song words and everyday language may reflect earlier forms that are retained in the song verses. He also argues that foreign verses are often imagined to have greater potency (ibid.:258) and he provides support for the argument that some of the language may be deliberately obscure in order to 'confound the uninitiated' (ibid.:71).

> The natives' oral traditions which provide the much-needed glosses for the elucidation of ceremonial verse varies greatly in quality . The atmosphere of secrecy which envelops the native songs is not conducive to scientific and grammatical exactitude. The older men jealously keep much of their knowledge from the younger men for as long as possible, and do not encourage the inquisitiveness of youth about the ultimate meaning of charms, observances and ceremonies. While precision in the material form of the couplets is rigorously insisted upon, the old guardians of the tribal secrets do not allow the younger men to ask too many questions (ibid.:197)

Strehlow's commentary on the words and sounds of the Ulamba (Rain) song of Inungamala draw attention to aesthetic features of its form that relate directly to the intention of the performers and the cultural and environmental context of Central Australia: 'It is obviously an incantation, sounding to our ears almost like despairing supplication, for rain in a country where rain means life, and where the cruel thunderclouds often keep drifting over the parched and eroded earth without shedding their moisture' (ibid.:95). Mauss had no material available that would enable him to understand the diversity of Arrernte musical performance and see how different emotions were expressed in the dialogue with totemic ancestors according to context and situation.

Strehlow is aware of the opposition sometimes drawn between prayer and magic. He was doubtless unaware of Mauss's work on prayer but he takes up the challenge of E. O. James. James draws a categorical distinction between magic and religion in terms identical to that of Mauss – where, if not separated and evolutionary, the latter is seen to be of a higher moral order: prayer refers to the transcendent order of reality external to man, dependent on a beneficent Providence as the highest God. James contrasts prayer to spells. Strehlow respectfully denies the distinction: 'it is in honour of the totemic ancestor, as well as for the benefit of the human beings who now inhabit the territory once made glorious by their power and presence.' (ibid.:332)

Much recent writing has focussed on the experiential dimension of Aboriginal religion and on the ways in which the ancestral dimension, often referred to as the Dreamtime, is manifest in the present (see e. g. Stanner (1966), Munn (1970)). While most attention has been paid to the role of myth, art and landscape in the creation of ancestral identity, the analysis of songs provides extraordinary insights into phenomenological aspects of Aboriginal religion. For example, an Arrernte word for 'compose' means to call out one's own name (ibid.:126), referring to the name of the ancestral being. Such data add to the more phenomenological aspects of Mauss's analysis, showing for example the way in which Aboriginal religious practice does indeed close the distance between the present and the world of the ancestral beings. Strehlow indeed argues that the song words become the names of the ancestral beings themselves and over time there is a conversion from descriptive attributes of place to proper names. Since each ancestral being has multiple names and multiple progeny associated with the place, the songs themselves comprise from some perspectives a sequence of names. The descriptive referent is only one meaning of the words, the other being the names of the ancestral being themselves. The naming function itself will influence the way the songwords are transformed over time, for example affecting stress patterns. To Strehlow the names are analogous to masks that transform the face of the person into the ancestral being. He concludes: 'If my theory about the masking character of syllabic redivision and musical super-stressing is correct then the rhythmic resources of Central Australia could be looked upon as being 'acoustic words' for supernatural utterances' (ibid.:129).

While there is an element of speculation in Strehlow's analysis it resonates widely through other Australian song traditions. In Eastern Arnhem Land Yolngu songs contain in addition to descriptive words in ordinary language sets of names that can be equally associated with ancestral beings, people and places. Those names have multiple referents and conjointly express aspects of ancestral beings and their relationship to events that took place at particular locations. An ancestral being may for example be associated with a yellow ochre quarry. The song verses may contain a number of different words all of which refer to the digging stick that he used to prize up the yellow ochre, all of which can be used as personal names. However, at other levels each name may refer to different aspects or attributes of the digging stick, for example the digging stick being carried or being thrust into the ground. This richer understanding of the semantics and aesthetics of song texts, rather than contradicting Mauss's conclusions that the language is the language of the ancestors, shows that language to be far more complex and semantically dense than originally thought. This creative dimension of Arrernte song is beautifully expressed by Strehlow when he writes: 'the gleaming light of the poetry transfigured the landscape of central Australia for the natives into a home fit for the totemic ancestors' (ibid.:382).

Research has revealed the complexity of Aboriginal religion and the fact that it is integral to their way of life as a whole and to the reproduction of society. Aboriginal religion has been shown to be a dynamic system of belief and practice that can adapt to changing circumstances and incorporate change. This no longer seems surprising yet at the end of the nineteenth century the complexity of Aboriginal society was scarcely grasped. Just as prayer in Christianity is performed in a variety of contexts from state assembly to individual contemplation, so too is the case with religious performance in Aboriginal Australia. The limited functional contexts that Mauss alludes to reflect the limited perceptions that European recorders had of Aboriginal society. Nevertheless something of the diversity breaks through. Prayer or its analogues are seen to occur at burial ceremonies, in initiation, at night before going to sleep, as part of corporate ritual or as individual expression.

His analysis provides insights that are productive ways of looking at behaviour even if his purpose is to differentiate Aboriginal practices from more advanced forms. Writing of the great water serpent of the Pita-Pita he notes that he appears detached from any particular local totem and appears in the rush of floodwaters to drown the imprudent.

> The wise person should speak to Karnmari and say something like this: 'Don't touch me, I belong to this country'. In short the words spoken here serve to inform the presiding

> spirit of the locality, to ask his permission to pass through it ... It should then be likened to all those permissions asked of local spirits (p. 76).

The connection between ancestral being, place and identity is something that has emerged strongly as a core theme of Australian religion since Spencer and Gillen's publications. As Strehlow notes: 'Everyone's genealogy has, as it were, been imprinted in the countryside, and the myth that mentions the name of his own conception site may be regarded as a birth certificate which entitles him to the religious ceremonies of the group, and as one of the legal documents which defines his social standing within his own community.' The concept of permission has become an important theme equally in writings about land ownership and religion (Williams 1986).

Conclusion

While it may be argued by some academics today that prayer is not one of those concepts amenable to cross-cultural discourse, since it may not be applicable or relevant to all cultures, the phenomenon that Mauss's extended concept would have covered has remained a neglected area of Aboriginal anthropology. The failure to use the term prayer in the hundred years that followed the publication of his work suggests its lack of salience to the many researchers who followed. But that does not explain the neglect of the oral rites of Mauss's definition. These oral rites have been written up under a variety of names: oral texts, song, poetry, incantation and so on, but seldom has there been attention to their form. The songs have been presented in terms of topic lists and the calling of sacred names as a punctuation mark in a ritual. But the whole point of prayer as Mauss understood it is the linking of form with content, is its expression of meaning; it is part of a conversation with God or spiritual beings in general. In the practice of Aboriginal religion learning and singing the songs is often said to be the central element; in Yolngu pedagogy, for example, the youth should learn the songs first before they can begin to understand the deeper meanings of things (see Morphy 1991). In women's mourning songs the song words express the emotional attachment of people to place and form a way of engaging others in their own emotional states (see Magowan 2001 for a rich analysis). The words are powerful through their sound and through their meaning and in their continuing use. Even if prayer cannot be used cross-culturally Mauss has drawn attention to a lexical gap in the interpretation of Australian cultures that covers those oral rites where relations with the spirit world are brought into being through words.

When I tried to persuade the Yolngu elder Narritjin Maymuru to teach me his Manggalili clan songs he was at first highly sceptical. He asked me how well I spoke his language, knowing the limits of my ability. He explained how he had grown up with the songs, had heard them on many different occasions and yet he was still learning more about their meaning. What hope had I? Yet the difficulty of the task of understanding and interpretation should be no absolute barrier. Indeed in this case it is a sign of how important the task is. The translations that have been produced by Strehlow and others demonstrate the richness of Aboriginal oral rites and yet in the end most translations and interpretations are likely to be produced collaboratively. Increasingly in parts of Northern Australia Indigenous Australians are themselves translating song texts into English in order to communicate the richness and complexity of the content of the verses to outside audiences.

References

Berndt, R. M. 1952 *Djanggawul*, London: Routledge and Kegan Paul.

Durkheim, E. 1912a *Les Formes élémentaires de la vie religieuse*, Paris: Alcan

Keen I. 1994 *Knowledge and Secrecy in an Aboriginal Religion*, Oxford: Clarendon Press.

Magowan, F. 2001 'Crying to Remember: reproducing personhood and community', in B. Attwood and F. Magowan (eds.) *Telling Stories: Indigenous History and Memory in Australia and New Zealand*, Sydney: Allen and Unwin.

Morphy, H. 1986 *Journey to the Crocodile's Nest*, Canberra: Australian Insitute of Aboriginal Studies.

Morphy, H. 1991 *Ancestral Connections: Art and an Aboriginal System of Knowledge*, Chicago: University of Chicago Press

Munn, N. 1970 'The Transformation of Subjects into Objects in Walbiri and Pitjantjatjara Myth' in R.M. Berndt (ed.), *Australian Aboriginal Anthropology*, Nedlands: University of Western Australia Press.

Spencer, W. B. and F. J. Gillen 1899 *The Native Tribes of Central Australia*, London: Macmillan

Stanner, W. E. H. 1966 *On Aboriginal Religion Oceania*, Monographs 11, Sydney University: Oceania Publications

Strehlow T. G. H. 1971 *Songs of Central Australia*, Sydney: Angus and Robertson.

Williams, N. 1986 *The Yolngu and their Land: A System of Land Tenure and its Fight for Recognition*, Canberra: Australian Institute of Aboriginal Studies.

Index

The index excludes references to the footnotes (in this English translation, the endnotes) of Mauss's *La Prière*.

Related Titles from Berghahn Books

Techniques, Technology and Civilisation

MARCEL MAUSS

Edited and with an Introduction by Nathan Schlanger
Published in association with the Durkheim Press

Marcel Mauss's writings on techniques and technology are at the forefront of an important anthropological and sociological research tradition, and they also highlight the theoretical and ideological challenges surrounding this field of study. A selection of Mauss's texts – including his major statements on methodology, on body techniques, on practical reason, on nation and civilisation, on progress and so forth – are here translated and presented together for the first time, with a discussion of their context, impact and implications.

This book will interest scholars and students dealing with the French sociological tradition, and also more generally those concerned with technology and material culture studies in archaeological, anthropological or contemporary settings.

160 Pages
ISBN 1-57181-662-3 hardback ca. $40.00/£27.00

www.berghahnbooks.com